G000298884

ENGLISH FOR BEGINNERS

hugo

English for Beginners

A Self-Tuition Course

Rosemary Border

Hugo's Language Books
www.dk.com

A DORLING KINDERSLEY BOOK

This edition published in Great Britain in 1998 by
Hugo's Language Books, an imprint of Dorling Kindersley Limited,
9 Henrietta Street, London WC2E 8PS

www.dk.com

© 1996, 1998 Rosemary Border
10 9 8 7 6 5 4 3

All rights reserved. No part of this publication may be reproduced, stored in a retrieval system, or transmitted in any form or by any means, electronic, mechanical, photocopying, recording or otherwise, without the prior written permission of the copyright owner.

A CIP catalogue record is available from the British Library.

ISBN 0 85285 291 6

This book is also available with a pack of two audio cassettes:
English for Beginners Cassette Course
ISBN 0 85285 292 4

Written by
Rosemary Border

Illustrations by
Timm Joy

Edited and designed by Naomi Laredo

Cover design: Colin Ely

Set in 10/12pt Palatino
by Intype London Ltd
Printed and bound by LegoPrint, Italy

Dedication

To guru Leslie, to editor Naomi, to artist Timm, and to husband John and son Hugo, whose software skills kept the whole project on course. Grateful thanks and love to you all.

Contents

Biscuits
my leg hurts!

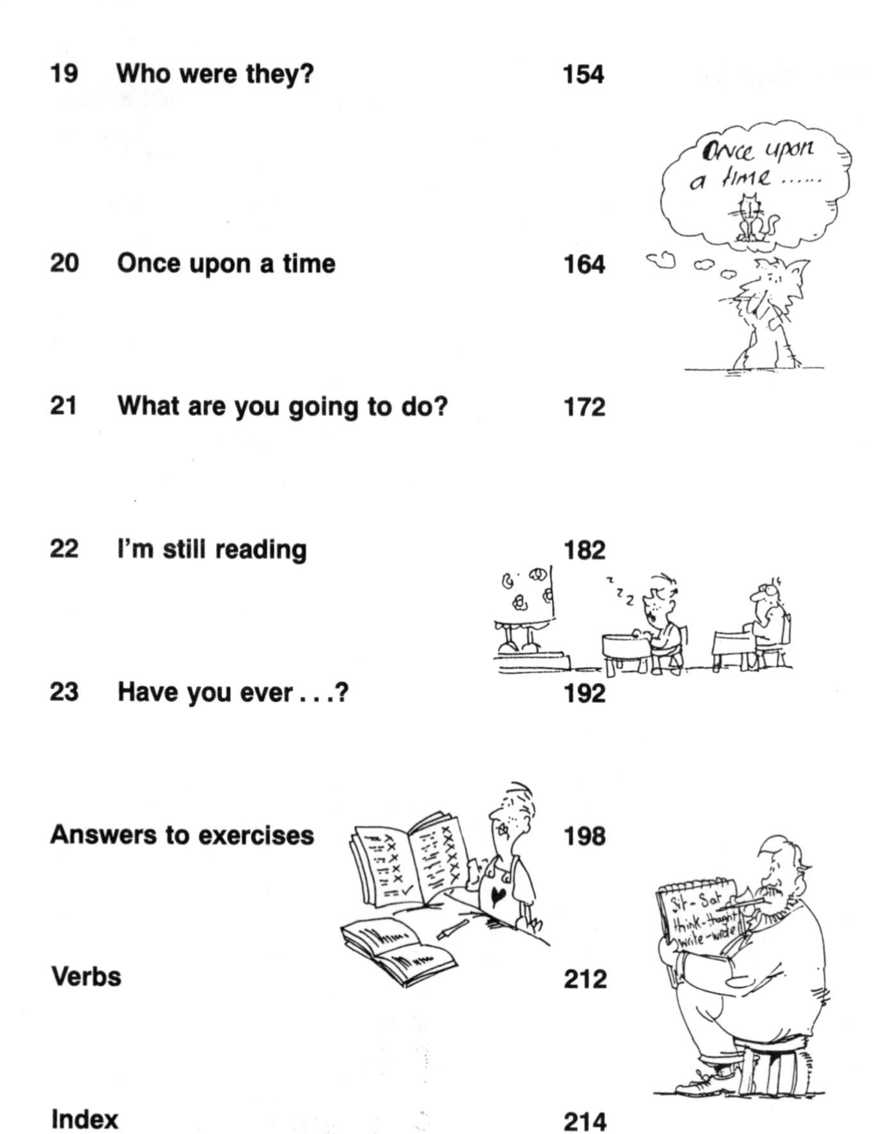

Once upon a time ......
Sit - Sat
think - thought
write - wrote

Introduction

Prof. English Hello! My name's English.
What's your name?

You My name's . . .

Prof. English Please write your name here.

My name is ....

Thank you. You need this book,
a pen, an exercise book, a table
and a chair . . . and some time.

You How much time?

Prof. English Half an hour every day is OK.
An hour every day is very good.
Good luck – and have fun!

1 Hello!

Hello! and Goodbye!

Prof. English
Hello and *Goodbye* are always OK.
We say *Good morning* in the morning.
We say *Good afternoon* in the afternoon.
We say *Good evening* in the evening. *Good evening* is like *Hello*!
We say *Good night* at night. *Good night* is like *Goodbye*.

How are you?

How are you?
Very well, thank you. How are you?
I'm very well, thank you.

How are you?
I'm fine, thanks. How are you?
Fine, thank you.

Thank you!

Do you know your letters?

an apple

an address

an aeroplane

an apricot

an artist

an author

a book

a boat

a banana

a cat

a cherry

a chalet

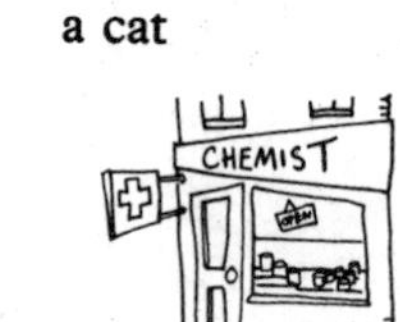

a chemist

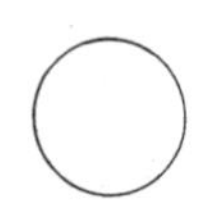

a circle

a cucumber

a doctor

a dog

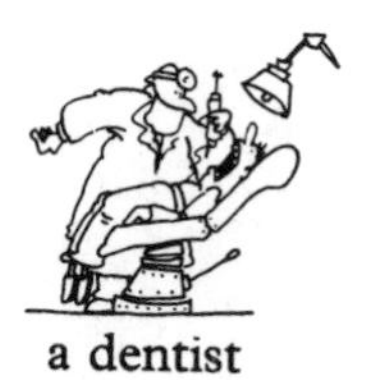

a dentist

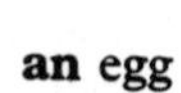

an egg

an ear

Earth

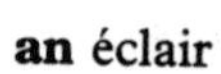

an éclair

an eel

a ewe

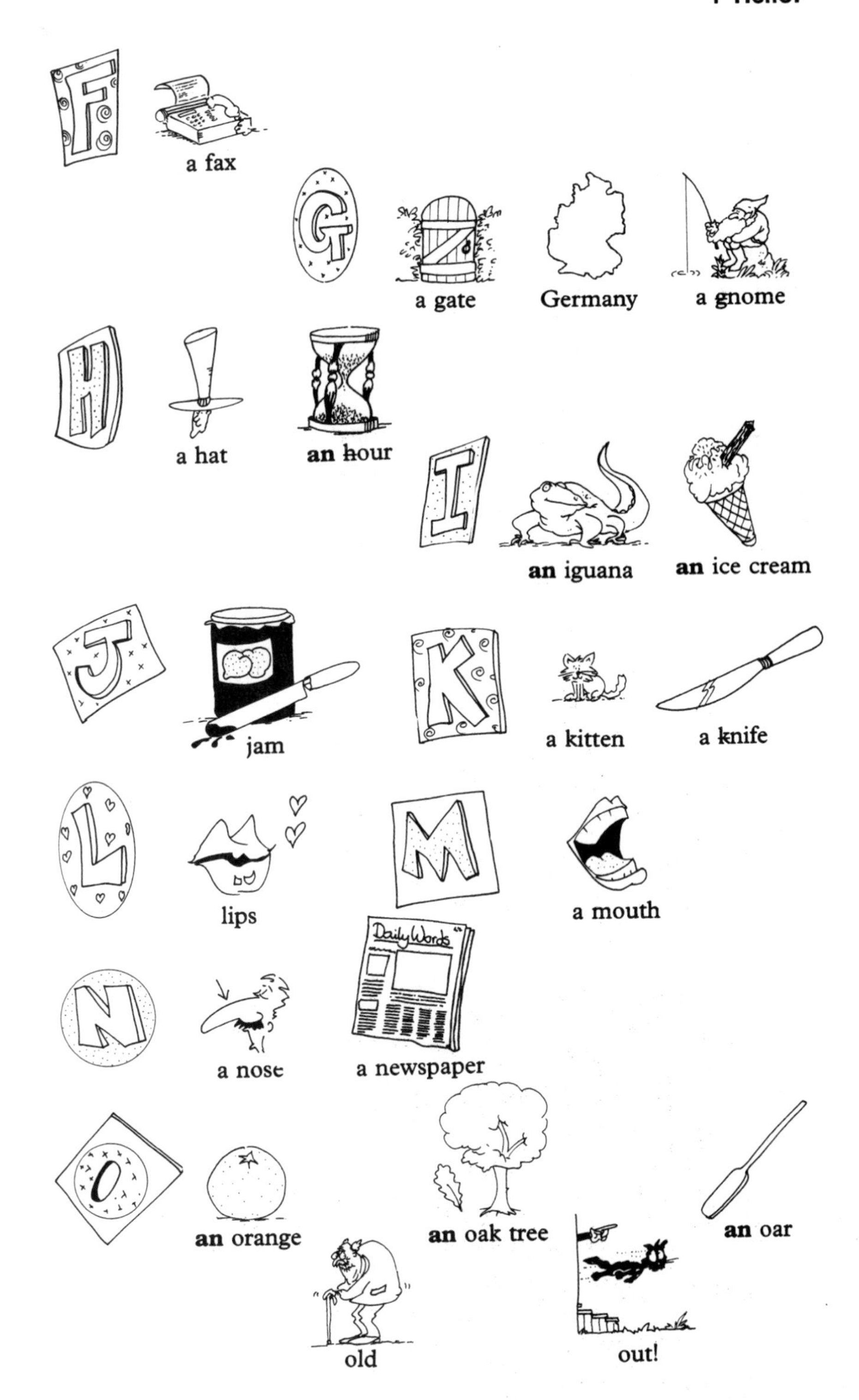
a fax
a gate
Germany
a gnome
a hat
an hour
an iguana
an ice cream
jam
a kitten
a knife
lips
a mouth
Daily Words
a nose
a newspaper
an orange
an oak tree
an oar
old
out!

P
a potato
a phone
a pterodactyl
Q
a queue
a queen
R
a rabbit
S
a sock
a sheep
T
a tooth
13
thirteen
this
U
an umbrella
an urn
a uvula
V
a van
W
water
writing
X
an X-ray
a xylophone
Y
1966
a year
Z
a zebra

Kit Hello! I'm a cat. My name's Kit. This is the alphabet.

Max Hello! I'm a mouse. My name's Max. This is the ABC.

Prof. English Alphabet! ABC! You're both right. These are the letters. We say: eɪ, biː, siː, diː, iː, ɛf, dʒiː, eɪtʃ, aɪ, dʒeɪ, keɪ, ɛl, ɛm, ɛn, əʊ, piː, kjuː, ɑː, ɛs, tiː, juː, viː, dʌbəljuː, ɛks, waɪ, zɛd.

Kit There are 26 letters in the English alphabet. Now what's this?

Max I don't know!

Kit It's the Russian alphabet.

I don't know

a and an

Prof. English We say ***a*** *book,* ***a*** *cat, a mouse,* ***a*** *xylophone*. But we say ***an*** *artist,* ***an*** *egg,* ***an*** *ice,* ***an*** *orange,* ***an*** *umbrella.*

Max And ***an*** *hour*!

Kit And we say ***a*** *uvula*. But we don't say it very often!

Prof. English That's right. Everybody has a uvula.

Max And we say ***a*** *ewe*.

Kit You?

Prof. English Don't be silly!

Prof. English Some letters are **silent**. We write them, but we don't say them. Max, say *gnome*.

Max Gnome.

Prof. English That's right, Max. Now say *hour*.

Max Hour.

Prof. English That's right. Now say *knife*.

Max OK, knife – now **you** say *pterodactyl*!

gnome

knife

pterodactyl

Prof. English
A E I O U are **vowels**. We say *an* in front of vowels. B C D F G H J K L M N P Q R S T V W X Y Z are **consonants**. We say *a* in front of consonants: *a cat, a pen*. But we say ***a*** *uvula* because in *uvula* the U sounds like a consonant. And we say ***an*** *hour* because the H is silent.

This is a letter.

These are letters.

Exercises

The answers are on page 198.

These are exercises.

A Write *a* or *an*.
Examples: *a* cat, *an* apple

. . . ewe; . . . apricot; . . . name; . . . day; . . . cherry; . . . artist;
. . . kitten; . . . cucumber; . . . dentist; . . . fax; . . . hat; . . . umbrella;
. . . hour; . . . mouth; . . . iguana; . . . year; . . . author; . . . uvula;
. . . queue; . . . ice cream; . . . ear; . . . rabbit; . . sheep; . . . apple

B Put the right letters in the spaces.
Example: ra . . it – ra*bb*it

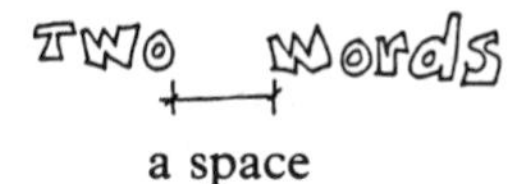

a space

d . nt . . t	q . e . e	wa . . r
ice c . . am	gno . e	a . . ress
ci . . le	. mbrella	xylo . . . . e
thirt . . n	o . . . ge	c . a . et

space

C Underline each vowel.
Example: cucumber

hat; fax; potato; van; lips; egg; mouse; circle; queue; dog; book; gate; orange; thirteen; zebra; teeth

D Right or wrong?
Write a cross (×) or a tick (√).

1. We say *Good evening* in the morning.
2. We say *Good afternoon* in the afternoon.
3. We say *Very well, thank you* in the evening.
4. We say *Good night* at night.
5. We say *Good morning* in the evening.
6. *Good night* is like *Hello.*
7. *Bye bye* is like *Goodbye.*
8. *Night night* is like *Good evening.*
9. *Good evening* is like *Hello.*
10. *How are you?* is like *Goodbye.*

E Put the right words in the spaces.

Rosy	.... morning, Professor. How .... you?
Prof. English	I'm .... well, ... you, Rosy. .... you?
Rosy	.... fine, ...

2 Names and numbers

What's your name?

Will Good morning. My name's William Shakespeare.

Man Shakespeare. How do you spell that, please?

Will S H A K E S P E A R E.

Man I'm sorry. Can you repeat that, please?

Will S H A K E S P E A R E.

Man OK, Mr Shakespeare. Thank you very much. What's your address, please?

Will My dress? I haven't got a dress.

Man No, no – your address! Where do you live?

Will New Place, Stratford upon Avon.

Man Catford?

Will No, Stratford.

Man Can you spell that, please?

Will S T R A T F O R D.

a dress

an address

Shakespeare My first name is William. My surname is Shakespeare.

Rosy My Christian name is Rosemary and my surname is Border. And my middle name is Margaret.

Prof. English My first name is Samuel and my second name is English. You can say *first name* or *Christian name*. You can say *surname* or *second name*.

Is your name Max?	Yes, it is.
Is your name Ken?	No, it isn't. It's Kit.
Is your name Posy?	No, it isn't. It's Rosy.

Prof. English Let's spell *Bobby Moore*.
You can say B O B B Y, M O O R E,
or B O double B Y, M double O R E.

Kit My name's Kit – K I T. Now spell your name.

Exercises

A Spell these names.

BOBBY MOORE; RICHARD WAGNER; MARILYN MONROE; LEONARDO DA VINCI; RUDOLF VALENTINO; ALFRED NOBEL; MOTHER TERESA; VINCENT VAN GOGH; CASANOVA; VICTOR BORGE; GERARD DEPARDIEU; MAHATMA GANDHI; MARIA CALLAS; BILLIE HOLLIDAY; JACK BENNY; ALBERT EINSTEIN; GEORGE WASHINGTON; ROSY BORDER; JOHN KEATS; XENOPHON; NAPOLEON BONAPARTE; MICKEY MOUSE

B Now spell these words.

book; fax; phone; zero; arm; aeroplane; writer; pterodactyl; X-ray

Numbers

11 eleven
12 twelve
13 thirteen
14 fourteen
15 fifteen
16 sixteen
17 seventeen
18 eighteen
19 nineteen
20 twenty

21 twenty-one
22 twenty-two
23 twenty-three
24 twenty-four
25 twenty-five
26 twenty-six
27 twenty-seven
28 twenty-eight
29 twenty-nine

30 thirty
40 forty
50 fifty
60 sixty
70 seventy
80 eighty
90 ninety

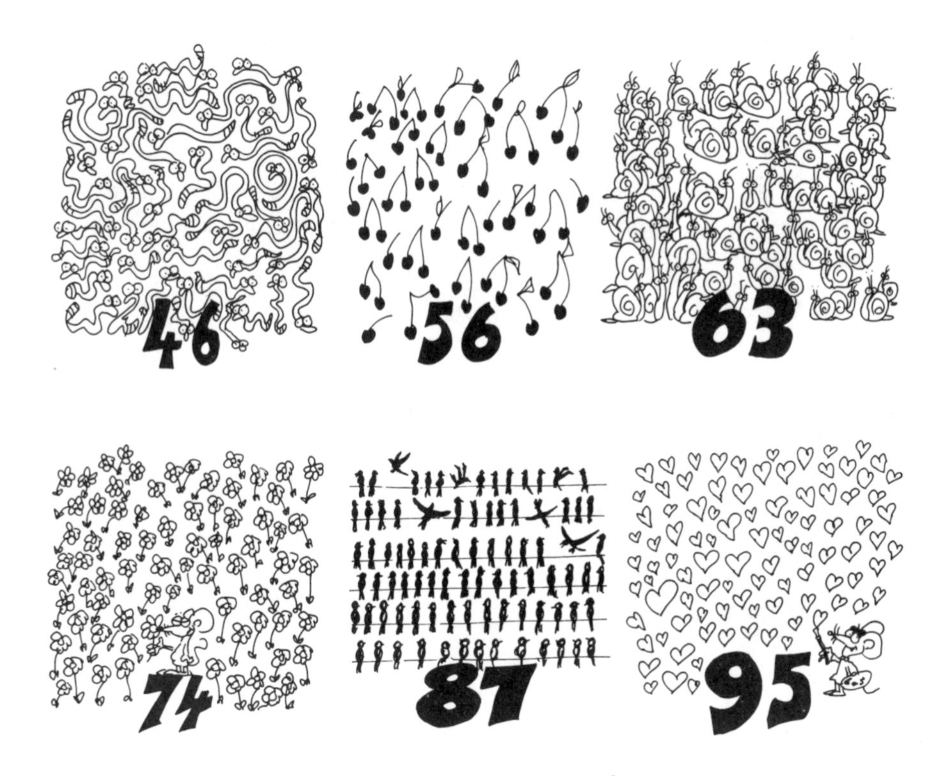

100 a hundred *or* one hundred
1,000 a thousand
2,000 two thousand
1,000,000 a million
10,000,000 ten million
1,000,000,000 a billion
3,000,000,000 three billion

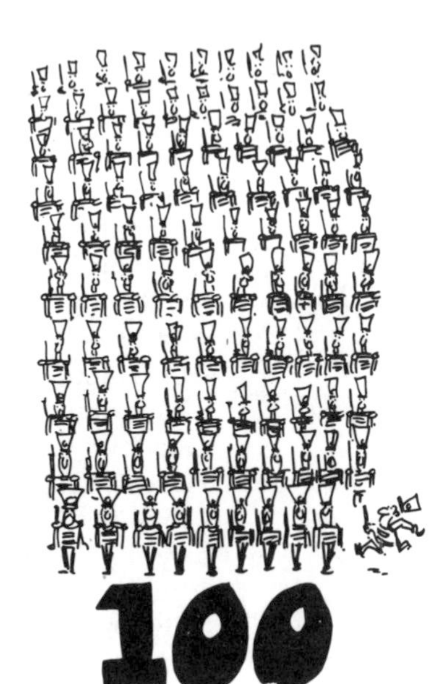

or

Exercises

C How many apricots?
How many cherries?
How many oranges?

D Write these numbers in words.
Example: 23 – *twenty-three*

4; 1; 17; 9; 20; 155; 42; 100; 184; 68; 76; 88; 220; 431; 709

E Write these numbers in figures.
Example: sixty-six – *66*

fifty-eight
one thousand two hundred and three
sixty-one
a hundred and twenty-four
eight hundred and nine
nine million
four
ninety
ten billion
twenty-seven

Hello! Hello!

Prof. English	0 1 3 9 4 4 6 0 2 9. Hello! Is that Rosy Border?
Man	No! My name's Jim Hancock.
Prof. English	Oh! Sorry, Mr Hancock. Is that 01394 46029 please?
Man	No. This is 01934 46029.
Prof. English	Oh dear! Can you repeat that, please?
Man	01934 46029.
Prof. English	Thank you, Mr Hancock. Goodbye. 0 1 3 9 4 4 6 0 2 9.
Rosy's voice on answering machine	Hello! This is Rosy Border on 01394 46029. Sorry, I'm not here. Please leave a message. Or send a fax. My fax number is 01394 42079.
Prof. English	Grrrr!

a message

telephone (phone) answering machine fax machine

Prof. English
Here's a telephone number: 441122. We can say *double four double one double two*, or we can say *four four one one two two.*
Here's another telephone number: 428910. 0 is *O, nought* or *zero.*
Here's another telephone number 213500. We can say *nought nought, zero zero, OO*, or *double O.* In James Bond books we say *double O.*

Exercises

F Say these phone numbers.

01473 25588
0171 400 424
0172 832832
0181 892 335
Now write them in words.

G Now say these car numbers.

H548DRT
N14WDX
A244FRG
C199EDG
L727BBM

H Now you!

What's your phone number?
What's your fax number?
What's your passport number?
What's your car number?

a passport

3 This and that

this and that, these and those

Is this/that a . . .?	Yes, it is.
Are these . . .?	Yes, they are.
Is this/that a . . .?	No, it isn't. It's a . . .
Are these/those . . .?	No, they aren't. / No, they're not. They're . . .

Prof. English	Hello! Is that a pterodactyl?
Artist	No, it isn't. It's a bird.
Prof. English	Oh. Sorry. Are those potatoes?
Artist	No, they aren't. They're sheep.
Prof. English	Oh, yes. They're sheep. And that's a dog.
Artist	No! It isn't a dog. It's a rabbit.
Prof. English	Are these apple trees?
Artist	No, they're not. They're cherry trees, and these are cherries.

What's this? What's that?

Exercise

A Put the right words in the spaces.
Example: 1 These *are* birds.

1 These .... birds.
2 This .... an ice cream.
3 That .... a boat.
4 Those .... apple trees.
5 .... these rabbits?
6 .... this an aeroplane?
7 .... those kittens?
8 .... that a passport?
9 What's this? .... a cat.
10 What's that? .... a sheep.
11 What are these? .... boats.
12 What are those? .... gates.

Who is this? Who's this?

Who is this?
It is Leonardo da Vinci.

Who is this?
It is Albert Einstein.

Who is this?
It is Napoleon Bonaparte.

Exercise

B Write *Who's this? What's this?* or *What are these?*
Examples: 1 Professor English – *Who's this?*
2 a queue – *What's this?*
3 rabbits – *What are these?*

1 Professor English
2 a queue
3 rabbits
4 Max
5 a banana
6 boats
7 an apricot
8 Madonna
9 birds
10 a ewe
11 cherries
12 Kit

Who is that? Who's that?

Who is that?
It is Madonna.

Prof. English
We **write** *That is an aeroplane; They are boats; It is a cat.*
We **say** *That's an aeroplane; They're boats; It's a cat.*
We **write** *It is not.* We **say** *It isn't* or *It's not.*
We **write** *What is this?* and *What is that?*
We **say** *What's this?* and *What's that?*
We **write** *Who is this?* and we **say** *Who's this?*
We **write** *What is your number?* and we **say**
What's your number?

Write	**Say**
it is	it's
they are	they're
it is not	it isn't / it's not
What is this?	What's this?
Who is that?	Who's that?

I'm a fireman

John is a fireman and
Harry is an engineer.

Brenda is a secretary.

Paul is a police officer and Sandy is a police officer too.

Shakespeare is a writer.

Della and Andy
are doctors.

Professor English
is a teacher.

Max is not a police officer. He is a reporter.

Write	Say	
I am	I'm	a writer.
You are	You're	a fireman.
He is	He's	an engineer.
She is	She's	a secretary.
We are	We're	police officers.
They are	They're	reporters.

Prof. English
1 = singular: This is a mouse. That is a mouse.
2 = plural: These are cats. Those are cats.

Prof. English
These are regular plurals:
1 boy, 2 boys
1 girl, 2 girls
1 reporter, 2 reporters
1 dentist, 2 dentists
1 cat, 2 cats
1 potato, 2 potato**es**
1 fax, 2 fax**es**
1 address, 2 address**es**
1 baby, 2 bab**ies**
1 cherry, 2 cherr**ies**
1 lady, 2 lad**ies**
1 secretary, 2 secretar**ies**

Look at this!

Prof. English
These are irregular plurals:
1 knife, 2 knives
1 person, 2 people
1 mouse, 2 mice
1 sheep, 2 sheep
1 tooth, 2 teeth
1 foot, 2 feet
1 man, 2 men
1 gentleman, 2 gentlemen
1 fireman, 2 firemen
1 woman, 2 women
1 child, 2 children

a foot

a person

a child

Exercises

C Answer the questions.

Examples: 1 Is Brenda a doctor?
No, she is not. She is a secretary.
4 Are Della and Andy police officers?
No, they are not. They are doctors.

1 Is Brenda a doctor?
2 Is Harry a secretary?
3 Are Sandy and Paul doctors?
4 Are Della and Andy police officers?
5 Is Professor English a reporter?
6 Is Max Mouse a writer?
7 Are Timm Joy and David Hockney writers?
8 Is Rosy Border an artist?
9 Is John a teacher?

D Ask the questions and write the answers.

Examples: 1 *Is* Brenda *a secretary*? Yes, *she is.*
2 *Are* Della and Andy *doctors*? Yes, *they are.*

a footballer

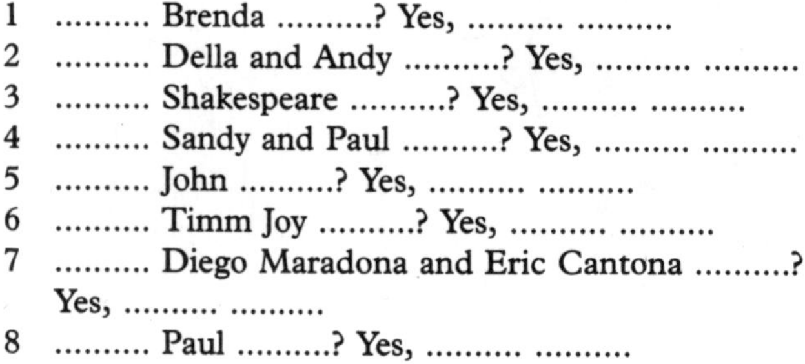

1 .... Brenda ....? Yes, ...
2 .... Della and Andy ....? Yes, ...
3 .... Shakespeare ....? Yes, ...
4 .... Sandy and Paul ....? Yes, ...
5 .... John ....? Yes, ...
6 .... Timm Joy ....? Yes, ...
7 .... Diego Maradona and Eric Cantona ....? Yes, ...
8 .... Paul ....? Yes, ...

E Who are they?

Example: 1 *This is Paul Newman. He is a film star.*

1 Paul Newman

4 Diego Maradona

7 Wolfgang Amadeus Mozart

2 Isambard Kingdom Brunel

5 George Eliot

8 Leonardo da Vinci

3 Madonna

6 Marie Curie

9 Socrates

film star	teacher	singer
author	composer	footballer
scientist	engineer	artist

F One mouse, two mice! Write the plurals.

1 One fireman, two ....
2 One lady, two ....
3 One tooth, two ....
4 One sheep, two ....
5 One baby, two ....
6 One tomato, two ....
7 One fireman, two ....
8 One chemist, two ....
9 One cherry, two ....
10 One foot, two ....
11 One mouse, two ....
12 One chalet, two ....
13 One fax, two ....
14 One letter, two ....
15 One person, two ....
16 One child, two ....
17 One knife, two ....
18 One secretary, two ....
19 One potato, two ....
20 One police officer, two ....

4 The Williams family

Meet my family

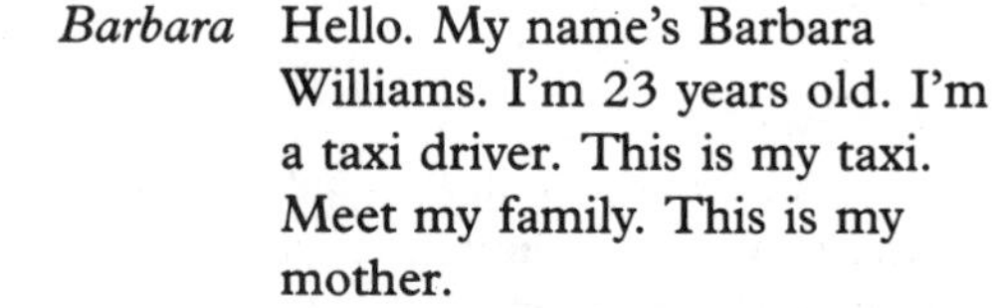

a taxi driver

a student

Kit's tail

Barbara Hello. My name's Barbara Williams. I'm 23 years old. I'm a taxi driver. This is my taxi. Meet my family. This is my mother.

Mrs Williams Hello! My name's Brenda Williams. I'm a secretary. This is my husband.

Mr Williams Hello! My name's Harry Williams. I'm 49. My wife's 45. I'm an engineer. These are our sons.

James Hello! I'm James, and I'm 17 years old. And this is my brother.

Charlie Hello! I'm Charlie. I'm 14. James and I are students.

James Yes, that's right. We're students. And this is our sister. Her name's Amy. She's ten.

Amy Hi!

James This is our sister Barbara. She's 23.

Barbara Hello!

James And this is Tim. He's Barbara's boyfriend. He's 23 years old.

Tim Hello!

Harry Williams = Brenda Williams

Tim Barbara James Charlie Amy

Mr Williams is **Barbara's** father.
He is **her** father.
Mrs Williams is Barbara's mother.
She is **her** mother.
Amy Williams is Barbara's sister.
She is **her** sister.
James and Charlie Williams are Barbara's brothers. **They** are **her** brothers.
Tim is Barbara's boyfriend.
He is **her** boyfriend.

Barbara is **James's** sister. She is **his** sister.
Charlie is James's brother. He is **his** brother.
Harry is James's father. He is **his** father.

Mr and Mrs Williams have four children.
Their daughters are Barbara and Amy.
Their sons are James and Charlie.

This is **Tim's** car, and this is **its** wheel.

Prof. English You can say *James and I are students,* or *We're students.* You can say *Barbara and Brenda are women,* or *They're women.*

Max One **woman,** two **women**. And one **wife**, six **wives**!

Animals, people and things

Max	Kit and I are **animals**.
Kit	Yes. We're animals.
Max	And men, women and children are **people**.
Kit	One person, two people.
Max	Books, pens and cars are **things**.
Kit	One thing, two things.

Mr, Mrs, Miss and Ms

Prof. English	Men are **Mr**. We write *Mr*, we say *Mister*. Married women are **Mrs**. We write *Mrs*, we say *Missis*. Girls and unmarried women are **Miss**. We write and say *Miss*.
Kit	Is Sandy Mrs or Miss?
Prof. English	Has she got a husband?
Kit	I don't know.
Prof. English	**Ms** is always OK. We write *Ms* and we say *Miz*.
Max	What about doctors and professors?
Prof. English	We write *Dr* or *Doctor*. We say *Doctor*. We write *Professor* or *Prof*. We say *Professor*.

married

Harry

Harry and Brenda

Amy

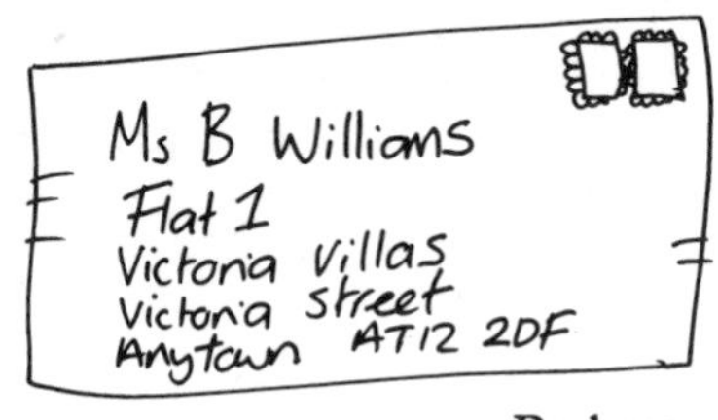

Barbara

Meet the apostrophe

the cat's tails

the cats' tails

Prof. English Meet the apostrophe. In *Barbara's address* **'** is an **apostrophe**. It means *of Barbara*. It goes **before** the s. *Barbara'**s** address; James'**s** brother; Charlie'**s** cat.*

Kit Apostrophes aren't important!

Prof. English Yes, they are.

Prof. English
Mr and Mrs Williams have two sons and two daughters.
Their daughters' names are Barbara and Amy.
Their sons' names are James and Charlie.

Look at the apostrophe. It is **after** the s. Mr and Mrs Williams have **two** sons. Their sons**'** names are James and Charlie.

How old?

young old

This baby girl is one year old. She is one.
These children are eleven years old. They are eleven.
This woman is thirty-four years old. She is thirty-four.
This man is a hundred and one years old. He is a hundred and one.
He is very old.

Prof. English We say *I'm twenty years old*. We don't say *I'm twenty years young*!

Kit How old are you, Professor?

Prof. English That's a **question**. How old are you, Kit?

Kit I don't know!

Prof. English That's an **answer.**

I have, I have got

Tim has got a car.

Brenda has a bicycle.

Rosy I've got an old car. It's a Peugeot and its number is H648DRT. Have you got a car, Professor?

Prof. English Yes, I have. It's a Rover. Its number is P697ADX. It's a new car.

an old car

Prof. English
We say *an* ***old*** *man* and *an* ***old*** *car*. We say *a* ***young*** *man* and *a* ***new*** *car*. People and animals are young, and things are new.

a new car

We say **he, she** and **they** for people. Rosy's got a car. **She's** got a car. Harry and Brenda have got four children. **They've** got four children. We say **it** and **they** for things. This is a Reliant Robin. **It** has three wheels. These are Rovers. **They** have four wheels.

Reliant Robin

Write	**Say**
I have a car. / I have got a car.	I have a car. / I've got a car.
you have / you have got	you have / you've got
he has / he has got	he has / he's got
she has / she has got	she has / she's got
it has / it has got	it has / it's got
we have / we have got	we have / we've got
they have / they have got	they have / they've got
I have not got a car.	I haven't got a car.
you have not got	you haven't got
he/she/it has not got	he/she/it hasn't got
we have not got	we haven't got
they have not got	they haven't got

Have you got . . .?

Prof. English Max, have you got fifty pence?
Max Yes, I have.
Prof. English Have you got fifty pounds?
Max No, I haven't.

Prof. English
Look at these questions! Now look at these answers!

Have I got 50p?	Yes, I have. / No, I have not/haven't.
Have you got 50p?	Yes, you have. / No, you have not/haven't.
Has he/she/it got 50p?	Yes, he/she/it has. / No, he/she/it has not/ hasn't.
Have we got 50p?	Yes, we have. / No, we have not/haven't.
Have they got 50p?	Yes, they have. / No, they have not/haven't.

Prof. English Now, Kit, please write a letter to Max.
Kit But I haven't got a pen!
Prof. English Yes, you have.
Kit But I haven't got Max's address!
Prof. English Yes, you have.
Kit OK, OK. But I haven't got an envelope!
Prof. English Here. Now write your letter, please.
Kit But I haven't got a stamp!

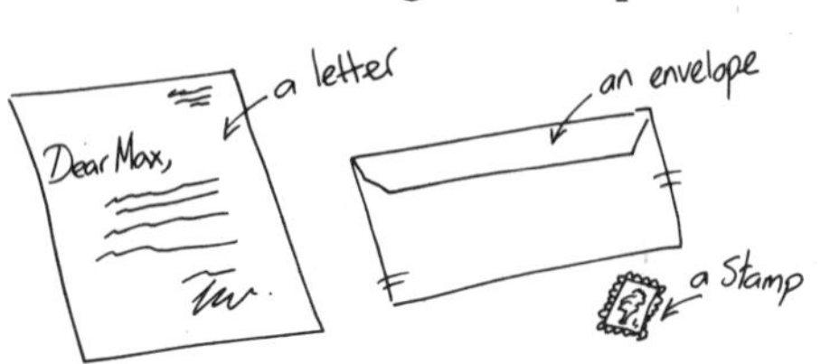

Exercise

A Put in the apostrophes.
Examples: Charlie*'s* address; the boy*s'* names

Professor Englishs address; the policemens cars; the dogs nose;
Harrys children; Maxs mother; my two sons names;
Barbaras boyfriends car; the three pterodactyls tails

B Write the answers.
Examples: Have you got a car, Max? *No, I haven't.*
Has James got a brother? *Yes, he has.*

1 Have you got a car, Max? (no)
2 Has James got a brother? (yes)
3 Has Professor English got an aeroplane? (no)
4 Have Kit and Max got tails? (yes)

my book, your pen
mine, yours

Prof. English We say *It's his, It's hers, It's mine, It's theirs*, but we don't say *It's its*.

Is this your car?

too, as well

This book is Barbara's
and this passport is hers too.

Prof. English You can say *as well.*
Max So *too* is OK and *as well* is OK too!
Kit And *as well* is OK and *too* is OK as well!
Prof. English Kit, you're silly, and Max, you're silly too!

This exercise book is James's
and this bag is his as well.

Exercises

C Write *my, your, his, her, its, our, their* in the spaces.
Example: I am a teacher and *my* name is English.

1 Charlie, have you got .... books?
2 This is Barbara and this is .... taxi.
3 These are dogs and these are .... tails.
4 Has Harry got .... hat? Yes, he has.
5 I am a doctor and .... name is Della.
6 This is a mouse and this is .... nose.

D Write *mine, yours, his, hers, ours, theirs* etc.
Examples: my book – *mine;* her taxi – *hers;*
Barbara's pen – *Barbara's*

your address; his 50p; their fire engine; my pen; Harry's car; our children; Tim's bag; your cat; my hat; her dog

5 Speaking and writing

who and whose

Who's this? It's Barbara.
Whose taxi is this? It's Barbara's.
Whose is this taxi? It's Barbara's.

Who's this? It's Tim.
Whose piano is this? It's Wagner's.
Whose is this piano? It's Wagner's.

Prof. English
Who's and **whose** sound the same. But they are not the same. And we spell them differently too. *Who's that?* is the same as *Who is that? Whose is that?* is the same as *Whose piano/helmet/car/ boyfriend is that?*

Exercise

A Here are the answers. Please write the questions! Write *Whose is this?* or *Who's this?* in the spaces.

Examples: 1 *Who's this?* It's Brenda.
2 *Whose is this?* It's Tim's.

1 .... It's Brenda.
2 .... It's Tim's.
3 .... It's ours.
4 .... It's Professor English.
5 .... It's theirs.
6 .... It's Max.
7 .... It's hers.
8 .... It's his.
9 .... It's Harry.

Two families

Meet the Clintons

a white house　　　　the White House

The USA has a president. His name is Bill Clinton.
His wife's name is Hillary Clinton.
The President and his wife have one daughter.
Their daughter's name is Chelsea Clinton.
The Clintons have a cat. Their cat's name is Socks.

Meet the Windsors

The British people have a queen.
Her name is Elizabeth.
This is the Queen's husband.
His name is Prince Philip.
Elizabeth and Philip have four children.
They have three sons and one daughter.
Their sons' names are Prince Charles,
Prince Andrew and Prince Edward.
Their daughter's name is Princess Anne.

Kit Has the Queen got a cat?
Max I don't know. She has six dogs.
Kit Oh dear!

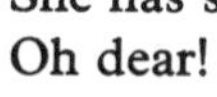

the

Prof. English
We say *This is **a** queen, and this is **the** Queen.*
*This is **a** white house, and this is **the** White House.*
*This is **a** family, and this is **the** Royal Family.*

And we say *This is **a** cat and this is **a** mouse.*
***The** cat's name is Kit and **the** mouse's name is Max.*

a king a queen

Those are firemen, and those are police officers. **The** firemen have a fire engine and **the** police officers have a police car.

Exercises

B Now write *Meet the Williamses.* How many people are there in the Williams family? What are their names? How old are they?

C Write about your family.

D Now write about your country. Has your country got a king? a queen? a president?

Barbara is dancing!

Prof. English What is Barbara doing? She is dancing. She is dancing **now**. Are you dancing, ... (please write your name here)?

You Yes, I am. / No, I'm not. I'm reading this book.

Prof. English What is Barbara doing now? Is she dancing? No, she is not. Is she reading? No, she is not. Is she writing? No. She is having a shower.

Prof. English *Barbara is dancing.* Grammar books call this the **present continuous tense.**

Prof. English	Max, what am I doing now?
Max	You're talking.
Prof. English	You can say – or write – *talking*, or *speaking*. I'm talking to you; or I'm speaking to you.
Max	But we say – or write – *speaking English*.
Prof. English	That's right. We don't say *talking English*. I'm speaking English now – and you're reading English.

dancing

having a shower

talking/speaking

Write

I am dancing.
You are dancing.
He/She/It is dancing.
We are dancing.
They are dancing.

Say

I'm dancing.
You're dancing.
He/She/It's dancing.
We're dancing.
They're dancing.

Write and say

Questions
Am I dancing?
Are you dancing?
Is he/she/it dancing?
Are we dancing?
Are they dancing?

Write

Answers
Yes, I am.
No, I am not.
Yes, you are.
No, you are not.
Yes, he/she/it is.
No, he/she/it is not.
Yes, we are.
No, we are not.
Yes, they are.
No, they are not.

Say

Yes, I am.
No, I'm not.
Yes, you are.
No, you aren't. / No, you're not.
Yes, he/she/it is.
No, he/she/it isn't.
Yes, we are.
No, we aren't. / No, we're not.
Yes, they are.
No, they aren't. / No, they're not.

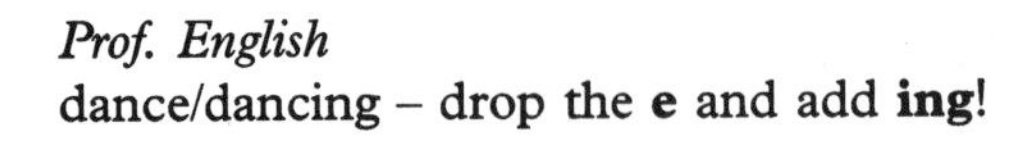

Prof. English
dance/dancing – drop the **e** and add **ing**!

wave/waving
ride/riding
drive/driving
write/writing
come/coming

dig/digging – add another **g** and add **ing**!
rub/rubbing – add another **b** and add **ing**!
swim/swimming – add another **m** and add **ing**!
run/running – add another **n** and add **ing**!
shop/shopping – add another **p** and add **ing**!
sit/sitting – add another **t** and add **ing**!

Here is a cat, and here is **another** cat.
Now there are two cats.

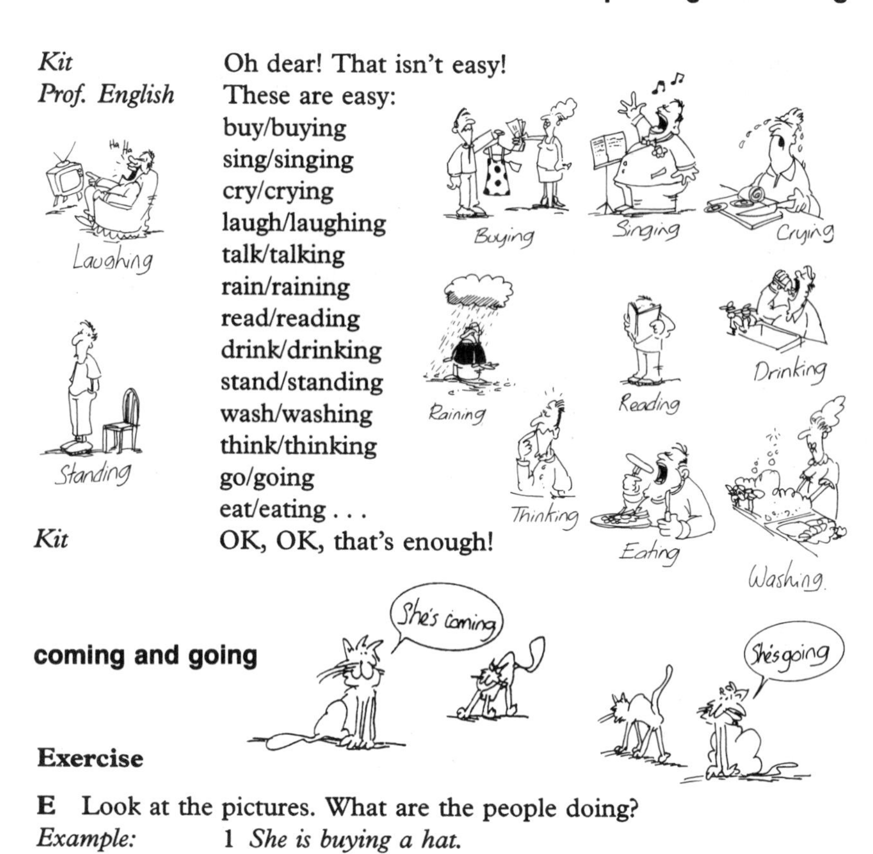

Kit Oh dear! That isn't easy!
Prof. English These are easy:
buy/buying
sing/singing
cry/crying
laugh/laughing
talk/talking
rain/raining
read/reading
drink/drinking
stand/standing
wash/washing
think/thinking
go/going
eat/eating . . .
Kit OK, OK, that's enough!

coming and going

Exercise

E Look at the pictures. What are the people doing?
Example: 1 *She is buying a hat.*

1 2 3 4

5 6 7 8

9 10 11 12

6 The time and the weather

What time is it? What is the time?
It is ten o'clock. The time is ten o'clock.

It is one o'clock.

It is five minutes past one.

It is ten past one.

It is a quarter past one.

It is half past one.

It is twenty-five minutes to two.

It is a quarter to two.

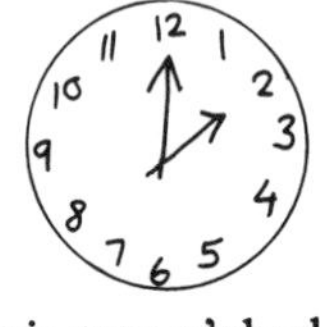
It is two o'clock.

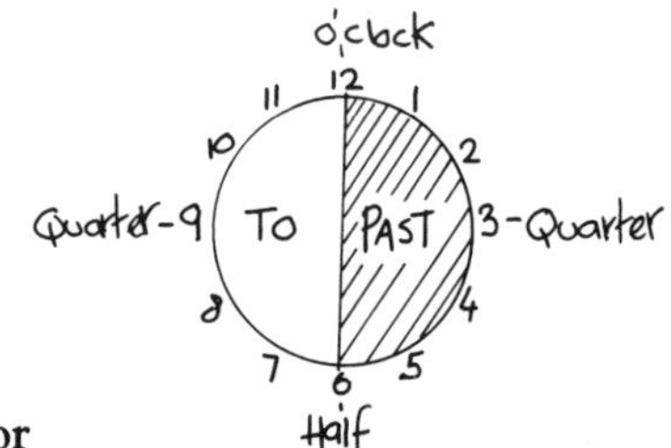

Prof. English We say *What's the time?* or *What time is it?*

Kit And the answer is *It is (one o'clock)* or *The time is (one o'clock)*.

Prof. English We say *Five minutes past one* or *Five past one. Ten minutes to two* or *Ten to two.*

Kit And we say *A quarter to two* or *Quarter to two.*

Max But we don't say *A half past one.* We say *Half past one.*

This is an hour.

This is a minute.

This is a second.

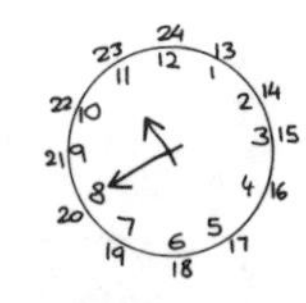

Prof. English	We say *Ten o'clock* ***in the morning*** or *Ten* ***a.m.***
Kit	a.m.?
Prof. English	*Ante meridiem* – before noon. **p.m.** is *post meridiem* – after noon.

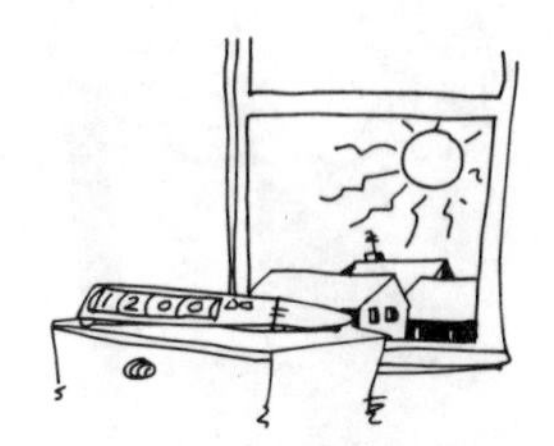

twelve noon

Write
What time is it?
What is the time?

Say
What time is it?
What's the time?

twelve midnight

The speaking clock

Barbara	What's the time, Tim?
Tim	I don't know. I haven't got my watch. Telephone the speaking clock.
Barbara	OK. 1 . . . 2 . . . 3 . . .
Speaking clock	Twelve fifteen and ten seconds. Beep, beep, beep.
Barbara	Oh dear! I'm late!

a watch

late and early

It is 6 o'clock in the morning. It is early.
It is 11 o'clock at night. It is late.

Barbara's morning

It is five minutes to six – 5.55 a.m. Barbara is asleep.

It is six o'clock. Barbara's telephone is ringing.

Barbara is awake now.

This kitten is asleep.

Now it is awake.

Barbara Oh dear! What time is it? Six a.m. OK, OK! . . .
Hello! Barbara's Taxis. Yes . . .

Man Hello. Oh, I'm sorry. Are you asleep?

Barbara No, no. I'm awake.

Man My name's David Duncan. I need a taxi at a quarter to seven, please.

Barbara A quarter to seven – OK! What's your address, please, Mr Duncan?

Man 23 Clinton Road.

Barbara OK, Mr Duncan. I'm coming.

Barbara is in bed. She is asleep.

Barbara is awake now. She is answering the telephone.

Barbara is writing Mr Duncan's address.

It is five past six.
Barbara is getting up.

It is eight minutes past six.
Barbara is having a shower.
She is singing.

It is twenty past six. Barbara is driving.

Barbara	Hello, Mr Duncan. I'm your taxi driver. My name's Barbara.
Mr Duncan	Hello, Barbara. You're early. Very good!
Barbara	Is this yours, Mr Duncan?
Mr Duncan	Yes, it is.
Barbara	Oh dear!

It is sixteen minutes to seven.

The weather

What's the weather like?
What's the temperature?

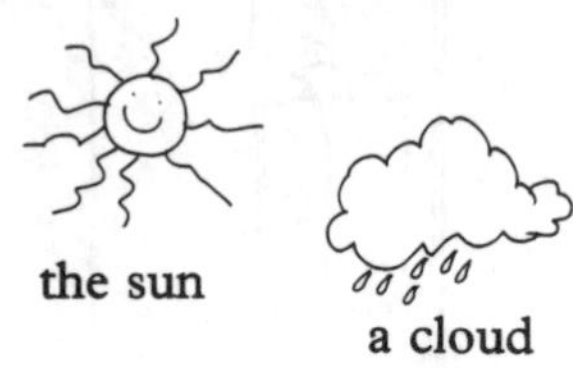

the sun a cloud

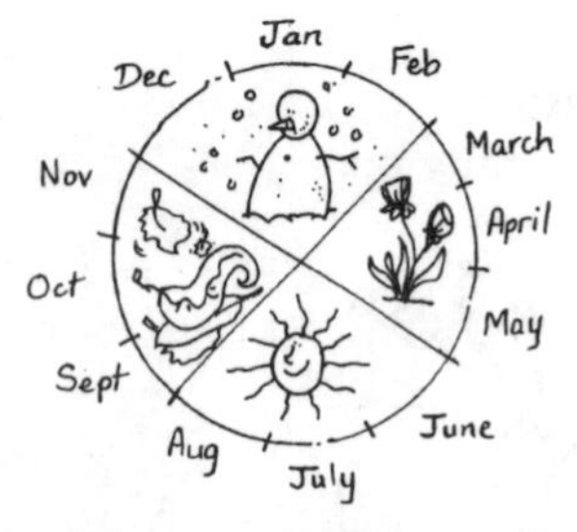

This is a year, and these are the seasons: spring, summer, autumn and winter.

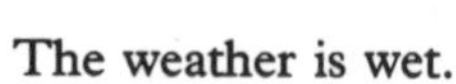

The weather is wet.

The weather is windy.

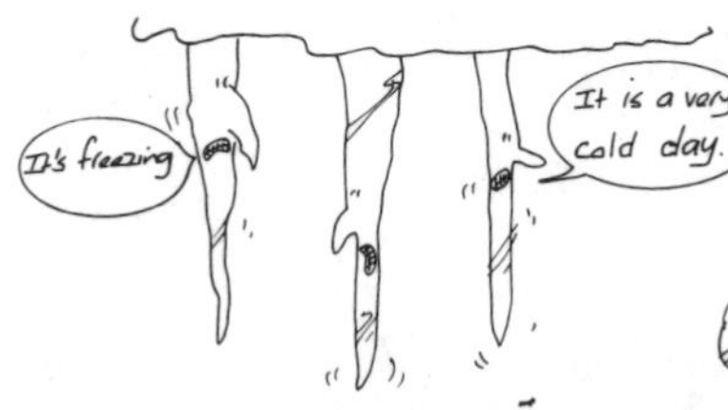

The weather is very cold.

The weather is cloudy.

The weather is foggy.

The weather is snowy.

The weather is dry and sunny.

An old song

Rain, rain, go away.
Come again another day!

come

come again

Prof. English We say *rainy, sunny, snowy, cloudy, windy* and *foggy*, but we don't say *freezy*.

Kit The temperature is nought degrees Centigrade. It's very cold. I'm wearing my winter coat and boots.

Max The temperature is 16 degrees. It's warm. I'm wearing my T-shirt.

Prof. English The temperature is 24 degrees. It's hot. I'm wearing my swimming trunks.

Jane Hello, Barbara. How are you?

Barbara Hello, Jane! Hello! I'm fine, thank you. Where are you?

Jane I'm in Spain.

Barbara Wonderful! What's the weather like?

Jane It's hot and sunny. I'm wearing my sunglasses. What's the weather like in England?

Barbara It's raining again!

Exercises

A What are they wearing? And what's the weather like?
Example: 1 *Barbara is wearing her coat. The weather is cold.*

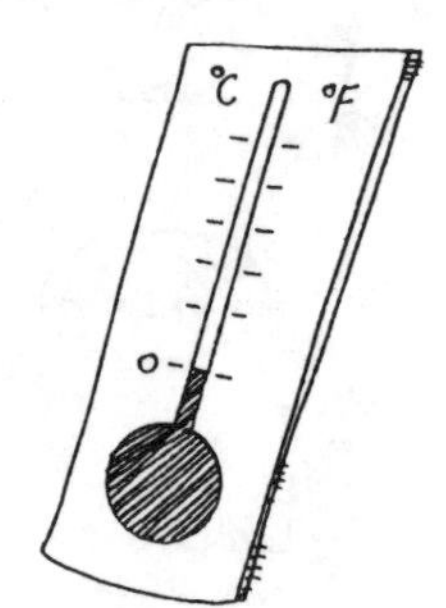

1 Barbara – coat – cold.
2 Tim – sunglasses – sunny.
3 Brenda has got – umbrella – wet.
4 Charlie and James – swimming trunks – hot.
5 Harry – big boots – snowy.

B Write these times in words.
Example: 1 2.15 *It is (a) quarter past two.*

1 2.15
2 7.45
3 9.35
4 10.11
5 12.30
6 1.12
7 8.47
8 4.55
9 6.50
10 11.05

The weather report

Barbara's telephone is ringing.

Barbara Hello. Barbara's Taxis.

Mr Duncan Hello. Duncan here. I'm at the railway station. I need a taxi now, please.

Barbara Yes, of course, Mr Duncan. Have you got your double bass?

Mr Duncan Yes, I have.

Barbara OK. What's the weather like?

Mr Duncan It's snowing.

Barbara Oh dear! Is it foggy too?

Mr Duncan No, it isn't.

Barbara Good! OK, Mr Duncan. I'm coming now.

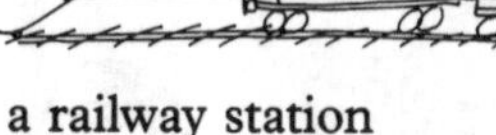

a railway station

an airport

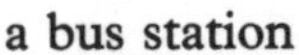

a bus station

Kit What are you writing, Professor?

Prof. English I'm writing notes. Look! "6.30 p.m. 15 degrees. Foggy."

Kit Oh yes! That's like "It's half past six in the evening. The temperature is fifteen degrees and the weather is foggy."

Prof. English That's right. Now you do it!

Exercise

C Write sentences.

1 6.30 p.m. 15 degrees. Foggy.
2 7.20 a.m. 30 degrees. Hot and sunny.
3 2.30 p.m. 4 degrees. Snowy.
4 11.20 a.m. 9 degrees. Very windy.
5 10.15 p.m. 12 degrees. Cloudy.
6 4.45 p.m. 13 degrees. Rain.
7 11.45 a.m. 22 degrees. Dry, hot and cloudy.
8 1.12 p.m. 0 degrees. Freezing.

7 What are you wearing?

Clothes

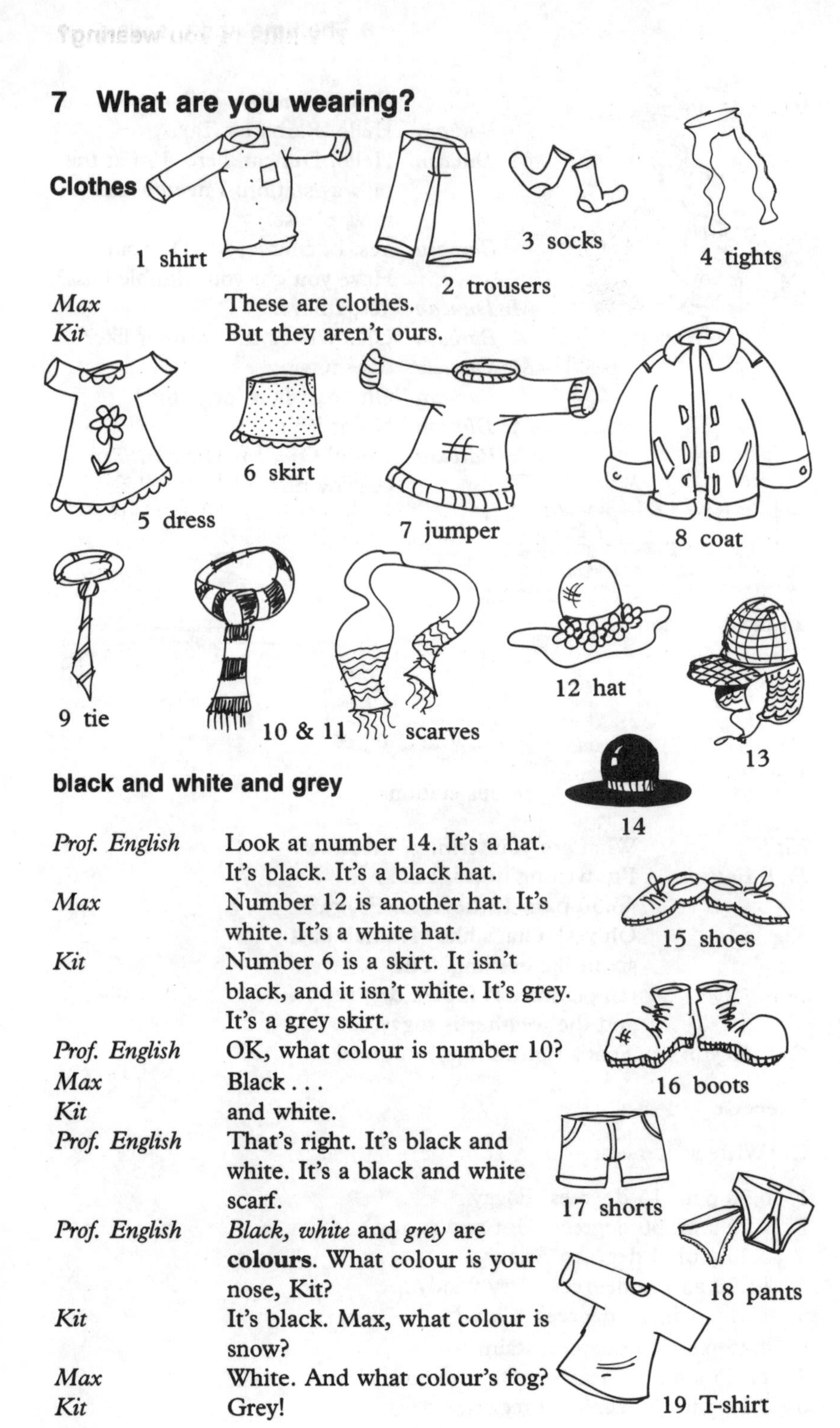

Max	These are clothes.
Kit	But they aren't ours.

black and white and grey

Prof. English	Look at number 14. It's a hat. It's black. It's a black hat.
Max	Number 12 is another hat. It's white. It's a white hat.
Kit	Number 6 is a skirt. It isn't black, and it isn't white. It's grey. It's a grey skirt.
Prof. English	OK, what colour is number 10?
Max	Black . . .
Kit	and white.
Prof. English	That's right. It's black and white. It's a black and white scarf.
Prof. English	*Black, white* and *grey* are **colours**. What colour is your nose, Kit?
Kit	It's black. Max, what colour is snow?
Max	White. And what colour's fog?
Kit	Grey!

wearing, carrying

Charlie is going to school. He is wearing a white shirt, a grey jumper, a black and grey tie and grey trousers. He is wearing grey socks and black shoes. He is carrying a black coat and a black bag.

Amy is wearing a grey skirt, a white shirt and a grey jumper. Her shoes are black, and her socks are white. She is not wearing her tie. She is carrying it.

Prof. English Charlie is wearing his tie. Amy isn't **wearing** hers. She's **carrying** it . . . Max, what are you carrying?

Max A fireman's helmet.

putting on and taking off

Kit It's cold this morning. I'm putting on my boots.

Max And I'm putting my boots on too.

Prof. English *I'm putting on my boots* is OK. *I'm putting my boots on* is OK too.

Max Phew! It's hot today! I'm taking my coat off.

Kit And I'm taking off my shirt.

Prof. English *I'm taking my coat off* is OK. *I'm taking off my coat* is OK too.

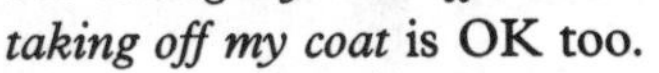

Exercise

A Make these notes into sentences.

Examples: 1 *Max is putting his boots on.*
2 *Kit is taking her hat off.*

1 Max – boots – on.
2 Kit – hat – off.
3 Barbara – dress – off.
4 Tim – shoes – on.
5 Professor English – shirt – off.
6 Tim and Barbara – T-shirts – on.
7 We – socks – off.
8 You – tie – on.
9 The firemen – helmets – off.
10 I – coat – on.

A pair of . . .

Prof. English This is a shirt and these are trousers. We say:
These are trousers, or
This is a pair of trousers.

Kit A pair is two!

Prof. English Yes, that's right. And I'm wearing a pair of sunglasses.

This is	a coat
These are	trousers shoes tights shorts socks pants glasses boots
This is a pair of	trousers shoes tights shorts socks pants glasses boots

Prof. English *We say a short dress* and *a short woman*. We say *a long dress*, but we don't say *a long woman*. We say *a tall woman*.

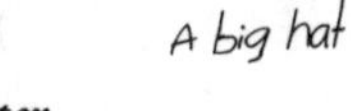

Reporter
Sally is wearing a long black dress, black shoes and a big white hat. Clare is wearing a short grey skirt, a black shirt and black boots. Martin is wearing black trousers, black shoes, a grey coat and a white shirt.

Prof. English
We say *This dress is long*, or *This is a long dress*, and we say *These trousers are short*, or *These are short trousers*, but we don't say *This dress is a long dress* or *These trousers are short trousers.*
Words like *long, grey* and *small* are **adjectives**.

glasses

Prof. English I'm holding a **glass**, and I'm wearing **glasses**. Another word for glasses is *spectacles*. And you can say *dark glasses*, or you can say *sunglasses*. But you don't say *dark spectacles* or *sun spectacles*. Look at Kit. She's wearing sunglasses.

Max But it isn't sunny!

Tim and Barbara

Tim's telephone is ringing.

Tim Hello! Tim King speaking. Who's that, please?

Barbara Hello, Tim. It's me.

Tim Who are you?

Barbara It's Barbara. How are you?

Tim Hi, Barbara. I'm very well, thank you. How are you?

Barbara Fine, thanks. What are you doing?

Tim I'm working . . . What are you wearing?

Barbara I'm wearing a short black and white dress, black tights and long black boots. I'm wearing dark glasses too.

Tim Super! What are you doing?

Barbara Guess!

Tim Are you painting your fingernails?

Barbara No, I'm not. Guess again!

Tim Are you drinking champagne?

Barbara No, I'm not. I'm driving my taxi . . . and now I'm outside your office. I'm waving.

Tim Oh, yes! Hello, Barbara!

saying and thinking

Tim is talking to his boss.
He is saying: "Yes, sir."
He is thinking: "You're boring!"

boring, interesting and exciting

James is reading an interesting book.
Charlie is reading a boring book.
Amy is reading an exciting book.

Prof. English — We say ***a** book*, but we say ***an** interesting book*. We say ***an** orange*, but we say ***a** big orange*.

Prof. English — These are inverted commas.
Kit — And this is a comma.
Max — And this is an exclamation mark.
Kit — This is a full stop.
Max — And this is a question mark.
Prof. English — Commas, inverted commas, full stops, question marks and exclamation marks are **punctuation marks**. Apostrophes are punctuation marks. Capital letters are punctuation marks too. In *Professor English*, the **P** and the **E** are capital letters.

Exercise

B Put in the punctuation marks.

Example: 1 *Tim is saying, "Hello, Barbara, how are you?" Barbara is saying, "I'm fine, thanks. How are you?"*

1 tim is saying hello barbara how are you barbara is saying im fine thanks how are you
2 whose trousers are these are they yours kit no they arent mine theyre maxs
3 mr duncan is telephoning barbara barbara is in the shower
4 hello kit whats the weather like whats the temperature are you wearing your boots

looking at, listening to, watching

Tim is looking at Barbara.
Amy is listening to a bird. It is singing.
The cat is watching the bird.
James is watching a film.

Prof. English We say *looking at*: Kit and Max are looking at me. We say *listening to*: I'm listening to my radio. I'm listening to music . . . We say *watching: watching TV, watching a film, watching a person*.
Kit! What are you doing?

Kit I'm watching that bird, Professor. I'm hungry . . .

Pronouns

Prof. English	I'm listening to Billie Holliday. She's a singer.
Kit	I'm listening to her too.
Prof. English	*Billie Holliday* and *singer* are **nouns**. *Her* is a **pronoun**. You know the **subject pronouns**: *I, you, he, she, it, you* (plural), *we, they* Here are the **object pronouns**: *me, you, him, her, it, you* (plural), *us, them*

Exercises

C Look at the pictures and write about them.
Example: 1 Tim *is looking at* an aeroplane.

looking at — listening to — watching

1 Tim an aeroplane.
2 Barbara and Tim TV.
3 Amy a bird.
4 Charlie is not the teacher. He his radio.
5 The people a film.
6 Brenda the children's dirty clothes.
7 James music.

D Write or talk about this picture.
1 What is A doing?
2 What is B doing?
3 Is C listening to the teacher?
4 What is the teacher saying?
5 What is D thinking?

very

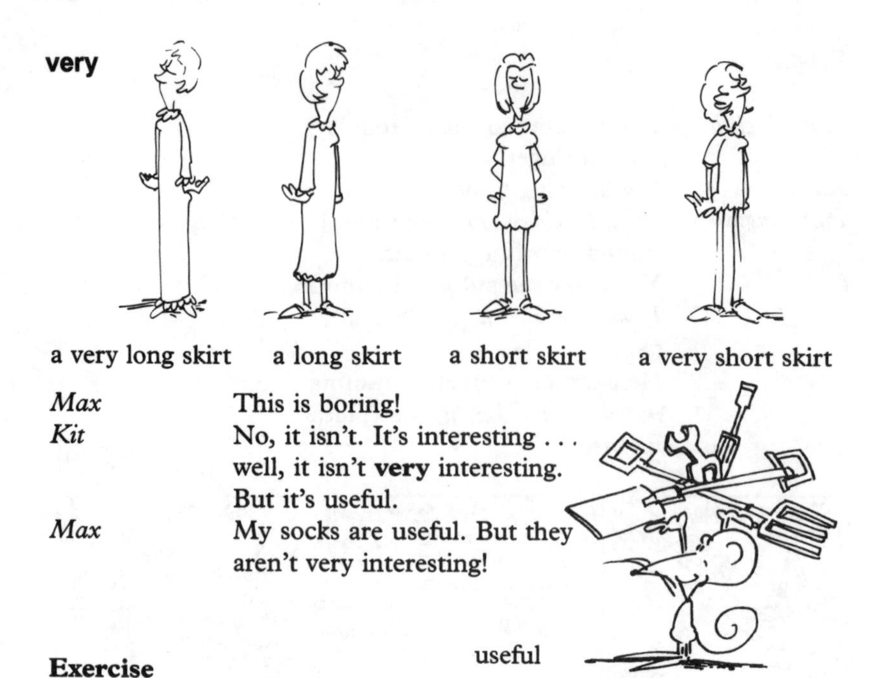

a very long skirt a long skirt a short skirt a very short skirt

Max	This is boring!
Kit	No, it isn't. It's interesting . . . well, it isn't **very** interesting. But it's useful.
Max	My socks are useful. But they aren't very interesting!

useful

Exercise

E What about these? Are they boring? Or are they interesting?

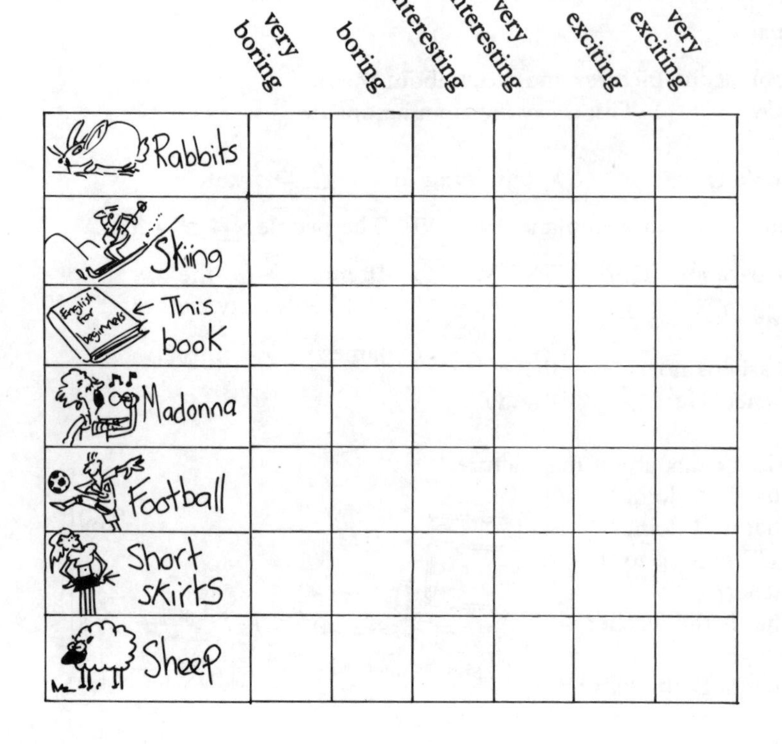

	very boring	boring	interesting	very interesting	exciting	very exciting
Rabbits						
Skiing						
This book						
Madonna						
Football						
Short skirts						
Sheep						

beautiful and ugly

nice and nasty

Prof. English	**Nice** and **nasty** are like *good* and *bad*, or *beautiful* and *ugly*.
Max	That's right. You're wearing a nice tie, Professor.

Exercise

F Look at these words and write sentences about them. Are they nice? nasty? useful? beautiful? ugly?

Example: *Umbrellas are useful. Kittens are beautiful, but they are not very useful.*

umbrellas; kittens; iguanas; taxis; oranges; long dresses; apricots; shoes; cherries; éclairs; ice creams; cars; trees

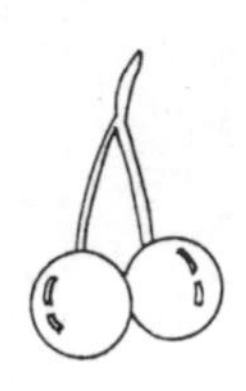   

8 Don't stop!

Do this! Do that!

Prof. English We say *Watch this* or *Watch.* We say *Look at me* or *Look*, and *Listen to that* or *Listen*; but we don't say *Look at* or *Listen to.*

Don't do this! Don't do that!

Starting and stopping

Mr Duncan	Stop the car, please, Barbara.
Barbara	What's the matter, Mr Duncan? You've got your double bass . . .
Mr Duncan	But I haven't got my music.

The policeman is stopping the car.

The car is stopping.

Prof. English We say *Stop the car!* or *Please stop talking!* Kit, stop playing and look at me, please.

Stop jumping! Don't jump!

Prof. English *look, have, sing, drive* – these are **verbs**. *I'm looking* is the present continuous tense of the verb *to look. Look at this, Stop jumping on the bed, Please don't eat that* are **imperatives**.

Max OK, OK, that's very useful.

Kit Yes, but it's very boring too. Now teach us something interesting, please.

no smoking

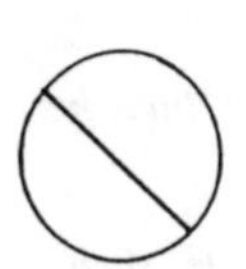

no parking

Don't eat it!

The mice are running away.
The cat is chasing **them**.

Barbara has got an apple.
Tim is saying "Don't eat **it**!"

Amy is hitting Joe.
He is crying.

Harry is mending a lamp.
James is helping **him**.

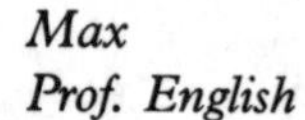

Max	Oh, it's those boring pronouns!
Prof. English	They aren't boring. They're exciting.
Kit	No, they aren't exciting. But they're useful.
Max	Cooking's useful too. Why aren't you teaching us cooking?
Prof. English	Because this is an English book. It isn't a cook book.
Prof. English	Now please do these exercises – that's another imperative.

cooking

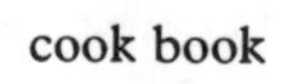

cook book

Exercises

A Write the pronouns in the spaces.

Example: 1 The mice are running away because the cat is chasing *them*.

1 The mice are running away because the cat is chasing ....
2 The mice are saying "He's chasing ....!"
3 Barbara has got an apple. Tim is saying "Don't eat ....!"
4 Joe is crying because Amy is hitting ....
5 Harry is saying "I'm mending the lamp", and James is saying "I'm helping ...."
6 Tim is helping Barbara. He is helping ....
7 The children are playing and their mother is looking at ....

B Write imperatives.

Example: 1 *Don't play football in the house, Charlie.*

1 Charlie is playing football in the house.
2 Amy is riding her bicycle on the grass.
3 Joe is picking the flowers.
4 Amy is jumping on the bed.
5 Barbara is singing in the shower.
6 Tim is parking on the grass.
7 Tim is smoking in bed.
8 The baby is pulling the cat's tail.

C Write *Stop . . . ing.*

Example: 1 *Stop playing the fiddle, Kit.*

1 Kit is playing the fiddle.
2 Max is singing.
3 Joe is playing football.
4 Amy is picking the flowers.
5 The baby is pulling the dog's tail.
6 Brenda is eating chocolates.
7 The baby is pulling the dog's ears.
8 The baby is eating the flowers.
9 Charlie is reading James's letter.

The days of the week

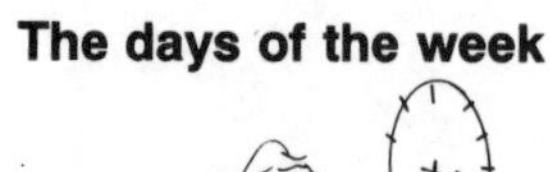

Monday

Tuesday

Wednesday

What day is it today? It is Monday. What time is it? It is half past three in the afternoon – 3.30 p.m. Tim is working.
Today is Tuesday. It is eight o'clock in the evening – 8 p.m. Tim is playing tennis.
What day is it today? It is Wednesday. What time is it? It is half past nine in the evening – 9.30 p.m. Tim is washing his clothes.
Today is Thursday, and the time is four o'clock in the morning – 4 a.m. Tim is asleep.
Today is Friday and the time is ten o'clock in the evening – 10 p.m. Tim and Barbara are watching a film.
Today is Saturday. What time is it? It is two o'clock in the afternoon – 2 p.m. Tim is helping Barbara. They are washing Barbara's taxi.
Is today Sunday? Yes, it is. It is eleven o'clock in the morning – 11 a.m. Tim and Barbara are cooking.

Thursday

Friday

Saturday

Prof. English	There are seven days in a week.
Max	We talk about **weekdays**.
Kit	Monday to Friday.
Max	And we talk about **weekends**.
Kit	Saturday and Sunday.

Sunday

The months of the year

Prof. English	There are twelve months in a year. The **first** month is January. The **second** month is February. The **third** month is March. In Britain, the first day of spring is the 21st of March.
Kit	Number one, number two, number three.
Prof. English	The **fourth** month is April, and the **fifth** month is May.

Max	Number four, number five.
Prof. English	The **sixth** month is June. The **seventh** month is July and the **eighth** month is August.
Kit	Number six, number seven, number eight.
Max	In Britain, July and August are summer months. In Australia, July and August are winter months.
Prof. English	The **ninth** month is September. The **tenth** month is October. It is autumn in Britain, but it is spring in Australia. The **eleventh** month is November and the **twelfth** month is December.
Kit	Number nine, number ten, number eleven, number twelve.
Prof. English	*One, two, three* are **cardinal numbers.** *First, second, third* are **ordinal numbers.** Some ordinal numbers are irregular: *one – first, two – second, three – third, five – fifth, nine – ninth, twelve – twelfth.* The other ordinal numbers are regular: *fourth, sixth, twenty-seventh* – you add **th.**
Kit	What about *eighth*?
Prof. English	You add **h.**
Max	What about *twenty – twentieth, ninety – ninetieth*?
Prof. English	You take off the **y** and add **ieth.**

Ordinal numbers

Figures	Words	Figures	Words
1st	first	7th	seventh
2nd	second	8th	eighth
3rd	third	9th	ninth
4th	fourth	10th	tenth
5th	fifth	11th	eleventh
6th	sixth	12th	twelfth

Kit	What's the date?
Max	It's the ninth of July.
Kit	Why are you wearing a paper hat?
Max	Because it's my birthday.

D What's the date?
Example:
1 *It's May the twenty-fifth. / It's the twenty-fifth of May.*

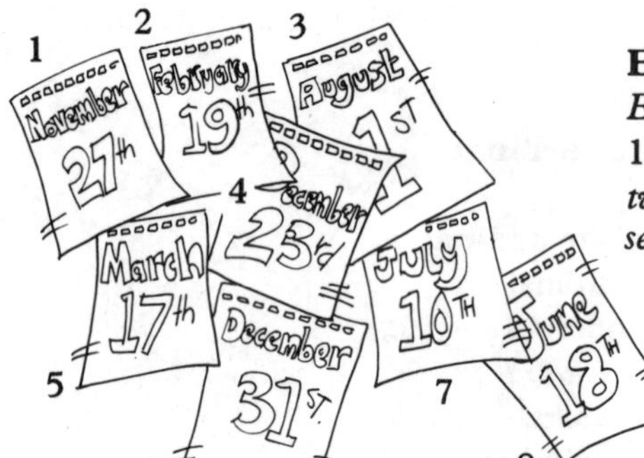

E When's your birthday?
Example:
1 *My birthday is on November the twenty-seventh. It's on the twenty-seventh of November.*

F What time is it?
What day is it?
What's the date? And what's the weather like?

Example:
1 *Good morning! It's 8.30 a.m. on Monday the twenty-fifth of August, and it's raining.*

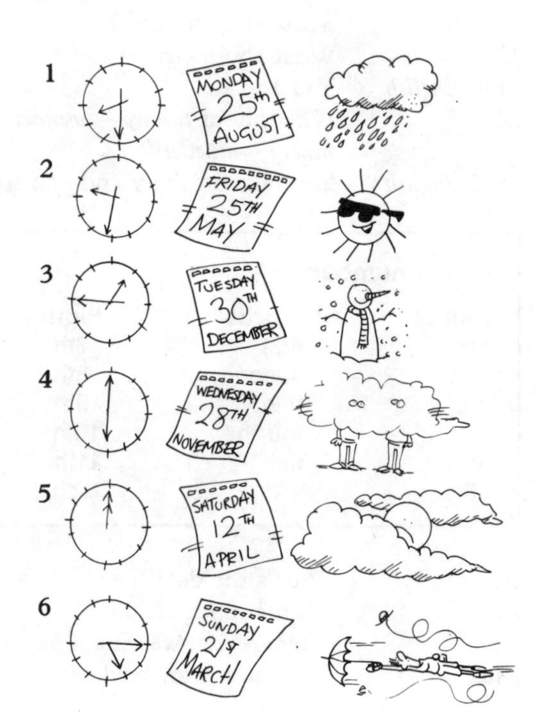

open and close

James is closing the door.

Max is opening the door.

Tim's eyes are open.
Barbara's eyes are closed.

This shop is open. This shop is closed.

A present for Barbara

Tim	Close your eyes, Barbara.
Barbara	OK.
Tim	Are your eyes closed?
Barbara	Yes, yes!
Tim	This is for you.
Barbara	For me? What is it?
Tim	Open your eyes and look.
Barbara	Flowers! Oh, Tim! They're beautiful! They smell nice too. But why are you giving me flowers?
Tim	Because it's your birthday.
Barbara	No, it isn't.
Tim	What's the date today?
Barbara	The ninth of June. And my birthday's on the ninth of August.

Prof. English **Smell** is interesting. We say *Barbara is smelling the flowers*. And we say *Barbara's flowers smell nice.*

Max We say *Tim's tennis shoes smell nasty.*

Kit And we say *This old sheep smells* – and that always means *This old sheep smells* ***nasty****. It's* ***smelly*** means *It smells bad.*

Prof. English OK, OK! I'm talking about pronouns . . . We say *Tim is giving Barbara a present* or *Tim is giving a present to Barbara*. But we **don't** say *Tim is giving a present Barbara* or *Tim is giving to Barbara a present.* We say: ***He*** *is giving* ***her*** *a present* or ***He*** *is giving a present* ***to her***. We don't say *He is giving a present her* or *He is giving to her a present.*

Kit That's very useful, Professor.

Max But it isn't very interesting.

Kit Eve's giving Adam an apple. What's she giving him? An apple.

Max Eve is giving an apple to Adam. What is Eve giving to Adam? An apple.

Eve Give me a kiss, Adam!

Adam Say "Please".

Eve OK. Please give me a kiss.

Prof. English *Max is writing a letter* is OK.
Max is writing to Kit is OK.
Max is writing a letter to Kit is OK.
Max is writing Kit a letter is OK.
But Max is writing Kit is **not** OK.

Tim is **sending** a present to his sister.
He is **sending** his sister a present.

Give me the ball!

Prof. English	*Give the ball to me* is OK, and *Give me the ball* is OK too. But we don't say *Give to me the ball.*
Kit	And we don't say *Give a kiss to me.*
Max	Why not?
Prof. English	I don't know. But we don't say it.

> Give it/them to me. Give me it/them.
> Give it/them to him. Give him it/them.
> Give it/them to her. Give her it/them.
> Give it/them to us. Give us it/them.
> Give it/them to them. Give them it/them.

Exercise

G Write the pronouns in the spaces.
Example: 1 Give *it* to *him.* Give *him it.*

1 Give the book to Charlie. Give .... to .... Give ....
2 Give the ball to Amy. Give .... to .... Give ....
3 Send these flowers to Brenda. Send .... to .... Send ....
4 Give those cherries to the children. Give .... to ....
5 We want those apples. Give .... to .... Give ....

9 The Williams family at home

The house

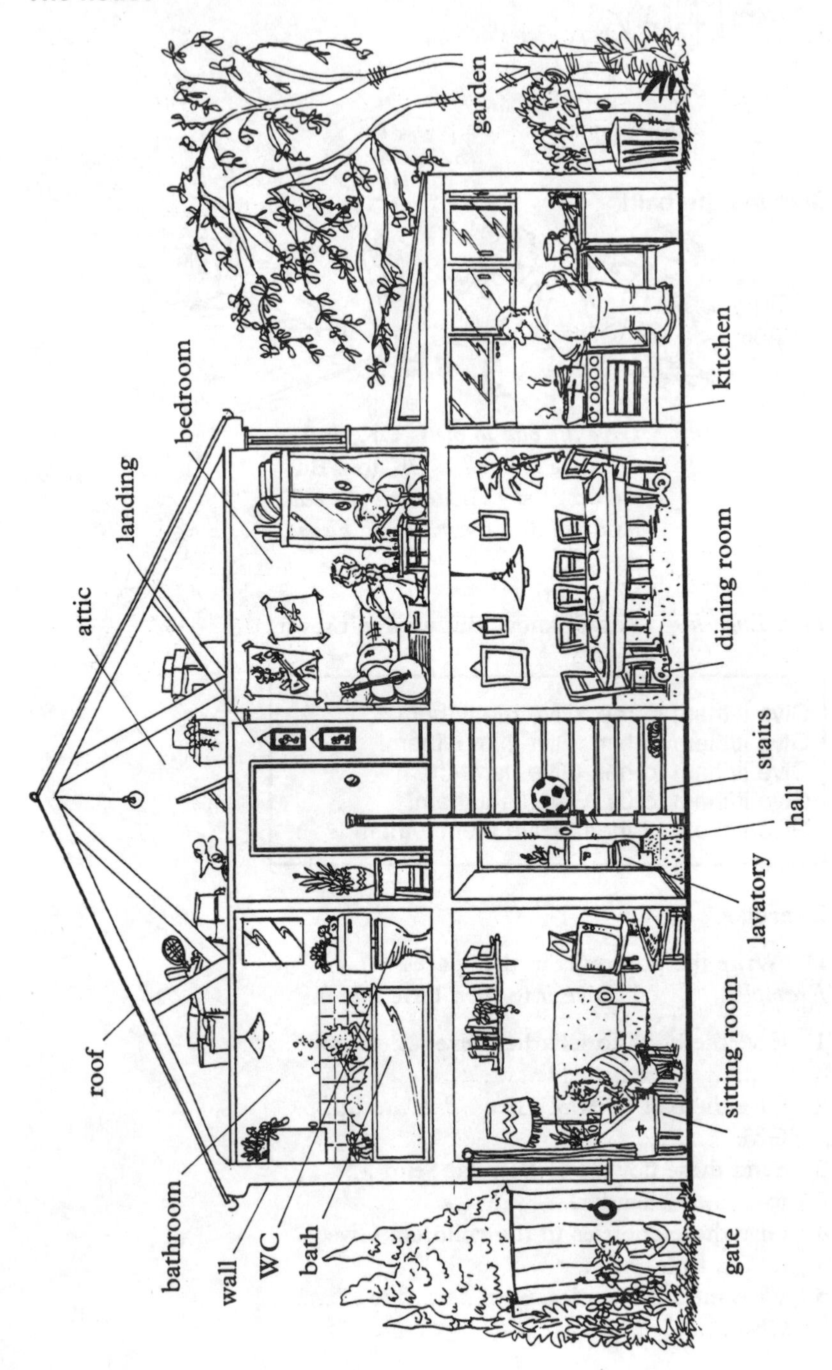

This is Mr and Mrs Williams's house. It has four bedrooms, a dining room, a sitting room, a kitchen, a bathroom and a downstairs lavatory.

Kit	Lavatory? I say *loo.*
Max	I don't say loo. I say *toilet.*
Prof. English	*Lavatory, loo, toilet, WC* . . . the Williamses have two – OK?

in and out
at home, not at home

Max is at home. He is in.

Max is not at home. He is out.

Where . . .?

Are the Williamses at home? Yes, they are.
Where is Brenda? She is in the sitting room.
What is she doing? She is writing a letter.
Who is she writing to? Her sister.
Where are the boys? They are in James's bedroom.
What are they doing? They are playing chess.
Where is Amy? She is in the bathroom.
What is she doing? She is having a bath.
Where is Harry? He is in the kitchen.
What is he doing? He is cooking.
Where is the cat? It is in the garden.
What is it doing? It is smelling the flowers.

Exercise

A Where does this go? Where do these go?

Example: 1 *Put the table in the dining room.*

dining room
downstairs lavatory
Amy's bedroom
James's bedroom
sitting room
bathroom
Harry and Brenda's bedroom
kitchen
Charlie's bedroom

1 table

2 armchair

3 sofa

4 cooker

5 bath

6 cupboard

7 Amy's bed

8 Charlie's bed

9 James's chest of drawers

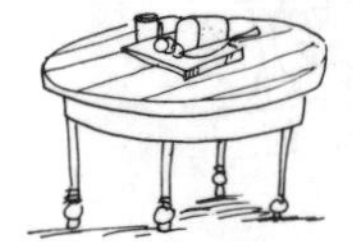

10 table

11 chair

12 wash basin

13 towels

14 dressing table

Playing

playing football

playing tennis

playing the piano

playing the guitar

playing chess

playing cards

playing a CD

Prof. English We **play** football, we **play the** piano.
Kit I'm playing the fiddle!
Prof. English *A fiddle* is an old word for a violin.
Kit There's an old song about me:
Hey diddle diddle,
The cat and the fiddle . . .

Let's play . . .

Max Let's play football, Kit.
Kit No, it's raining. Let's play chess.
Max OK.

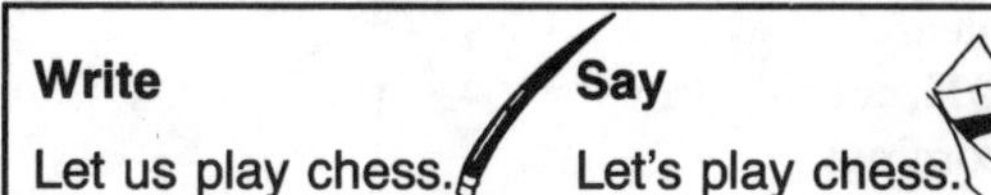

Tim and Barbara

tired

Barbara Let's go out, Tim!
Tim No, I'm tired. Let's watch TV.
Barbara Well, let's have a drink.
Tim I'm not thirsty.
Barbara Let's have dinner.
Tim I'm not hungry.
Barbara You're boring, Tim! I'm going out. Goodbye.
Tim Barbara?
Barbara Yes, Tim?
Tim Close the door, please!

Exercise

B Write sentences.
Example: 1 *Let's watch TV. No, let's play football.*

1 (watch TV). (play football).
2 (have a drink). (play chess).
3 (listen to the radio). (play cards).
4 (have dinner). (dance).
5 (dig the garden). (play the xylophone).
6 (wash the car). (drink champagne).

here and there

Prof. English Kit's here, and Max is there.
Kit Where's Max?
Prof. English He's there. Come here, Max.
Max OK, I'm coming!

Brenda is looking for Amy.
Brenda Where's Amy? She isn't here. Charlie, where's Amy?
Charlie She's over there, mum.
Amy I'm here, mum. I'm in my tree house!
Brenda Well, come here, please!
Amy OK, mum – I'm coming!

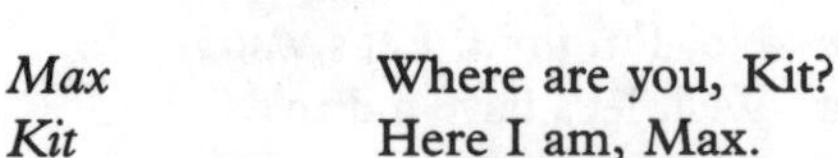

Max Where are you, Kit?
Kit Here I am, Max.
Prof. English *I'm here* is OK. *Here I am* is OK too . . . Where's that cat?
Max There he is, Professor.

looking for

Prof. English I'm looking for my glasses. Where are they?
Kit Here they are, Professor. I've got them.
Prof. English Thank you, Kit.
Look at and *Look for* are two different verbs.
I'm **looking at** you, and now I'm **looking for** my pen. Where is it?
Max Here it is, Professor.

in, on, under

Tim is **in** Barbara's car.
Barbara's spanner is **on** the seat.
Barbara is **under** the car.

spanner

seat

mending

Barbara Where's my spanner?
Tim It's here, on the seat.
Barbara Give it to me, please.
Tim OK. Here you are.
Barbara Thanks.
Brenda Hello, Tim. Where's Barbara?
Barbara I'm here, mum.
Brenda Where's "here"?
Tim She's under the car, Mrs Williams.
Brenda What's she doing?
Barbara I'm playing the piano.
Brenda Well . . .! What **is** she doing, Tim?
Tim She's mending the car, Mrs Williams, and I'm helping her.

up and down

Amy is climbing **up**.
Amy is climbing **down**.
The lift is going **up**.
The lift is going **down**.

Prof. English We say *climbing up*, but we talk about *climbing Mont Blanc* or *climbing trees* – we don't say *up*.
Max Let's climb Mount Everest!
Kit Why?
Max Because it's there!

in and out

Mr Duncan is coming **out of** his house. He is coming **out**.
He is putting his double bass **into** the taxi. He is putting it **in**.
He is getting **into** Barbara's taxi. He is getting **in**.
Mr Duncan is getting **out of** the taxi. He is getting **out**.
Now Mr Duncan is taking the double bass **out of** the taxi. He is taking it **out**.
He is going **into** the concert hall. He is going **in**.

concert hall

onto and on

The cat is jumping **onto** the table.

Now it is **on** the table. It is eating a chicken.

Prof. English
We say *I'm going* ***into*** *the house* or *I'm going* ***in***. We don't say *I'm going into.* We say *I'm coming* ***out*** *of the house* or *I'm coming* ***out***. We don't say *I'm coming out of.* We say *The cat's jumping* ***onto*** *the table* or *It's jumping* ***on***. We don't say *It's jumping onto.*

upstairs, downstairs

Exercises

C Where are they? Write the numbers on the picture.

1 Harry is in the armchair.
2 Harry's glasses are on the table.
3 Brenda is on the sofa.
4 Charlie is coming in.
5 James is looking out of the window.
6 There is a newspaper under the table.
7 There is a picture on the wall.

D What is this? What are these? Whose is this? Whose are these?
Look at the pictures and answer the questions.
Example: 1 *These are football boots. They are Charlie's.*

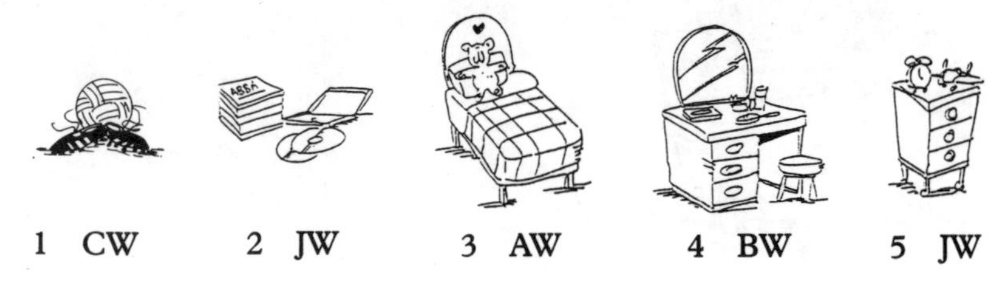

1 CW 2 JW 3 AW 4 BW 5 JW

10 What colour is it?

there is, there are

Look again at the picture of the house on page 76. There is a table in the dining room. How many chairs are there? There are six chairs in the dining room. There are six plates on the table. There is a cooker in the kitchen. There are cupboards too. Is there a carpet on the floor? No, there is not.

Carpet

Prof. English We say ***There is** a sofa*, but we say ***There are** four chairs.*
How many days are there in November?
How many hours are there in a day?
How many pages are there in this book?

The fly

Man Look! There's a fly in my soup.
Woman Oh dear! Yes, there is. Waiter!
Waiter Yes, madam?
Woman What's this fly doing in my husband's soup?
Waiter It's swimming, madam.

Max Waiter, there's a fly in my soup.
Kit It's OK, sir; the soup isn't hot.

Rosy's village

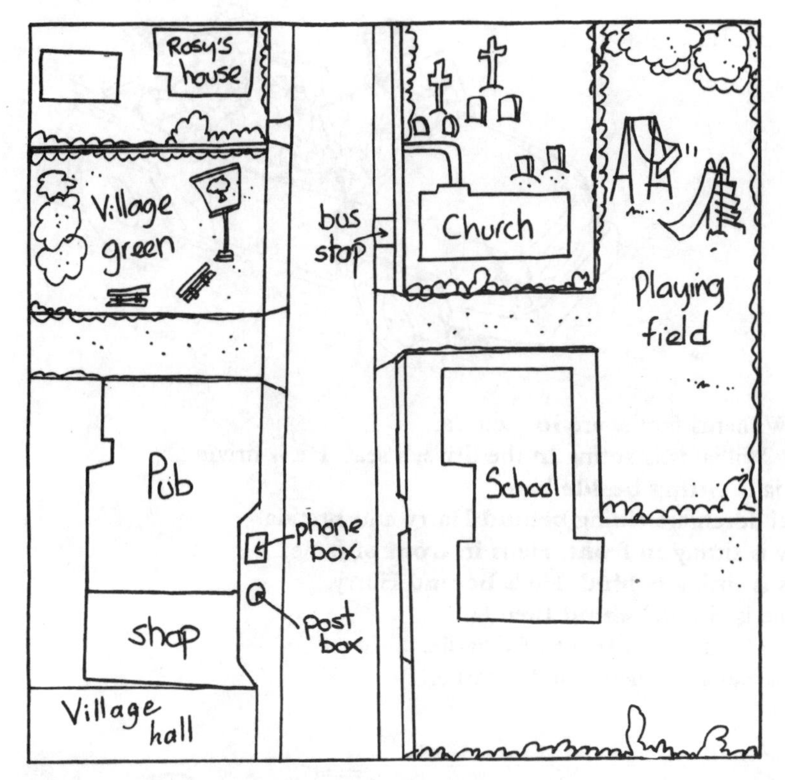

Rosy's house is in Eyke. Eyke is a small, quiet village. There are fields, woods and gardens. There is a playing field. There is a small grey church in the middle of the village. There is a very old pub called The Elephant and Castle.

There is a shop called Eyke Village Stores. It is a post office too, and there is a post box outside. There is an old red telephone box too. There is a bus stop. There is a village hall, but there isn't a cinema or a concert hall.

There is a school called Eyke First School. There are benches on the village green. Eyke has a village sign with a picture of an oak tree: Eyke is an old word for "oak". And yes, there **are** oak trees on the village green.

beside, in front of, behind, between

The Williams family are **in** their car.
Harry Williams is sitting **in** the driver's seat. He is driving.
Brenda is **sitting beside** him.
The children are sitting **behind** Harry and Brenda.
Harry is sitting **in front**. He is **in front of** James.
James is sitting **behind**. He is **behind** Harry.
Charlie is sitting **behind** Brenda.
Brenda is sitting **in front of** Charlie.
Amy is **between** James and Charlie.

on a chair

in a seat

the front

the back

inside, outside

The woman is **outside** the house. She is **outside**.
The man is **inside** the house. He is **inside**.

Now the man is **outside** and the woman is **inside**.

Exercises

A Look at the picture of the car again for thirty seconds. Then close the book and write answers to these questions.

Example: 1 *Brenda is sitting in front of Charlie.*

1. Who is sitting in front of Charlie?
2. Who is sitting beside Harry?
3. Who is in the driver's seat?
4. What is Brenda doing?
5. Is Harry talking?
6. Who is sitting between James and Charlie?
7. What is Harry doing?
8. What is Charlie wearing on his head?

B Write about this picture.

Example: *There are two boys in front of the village sign. They are playing football.*

Colours

Prof. English This is the United States of America.
Max The USA.
Prof. English And this is the American flag. It is red, white and blue.

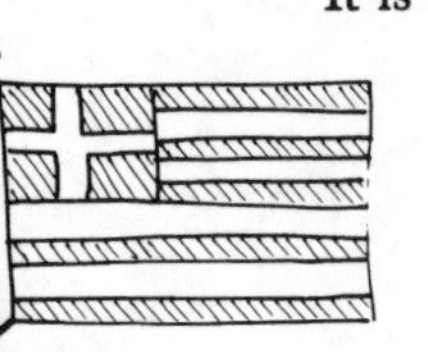

This is the Greek flag.
It is blue and white.

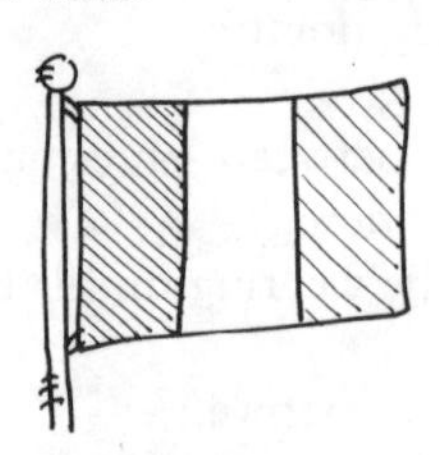

This is the French flag.
It is red, white and blue.

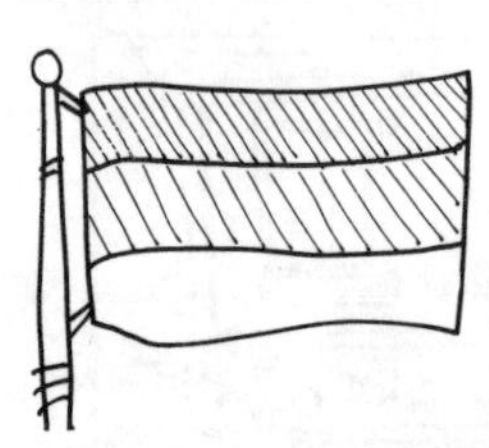

What colour is the German flag?
Black, red and yellow.

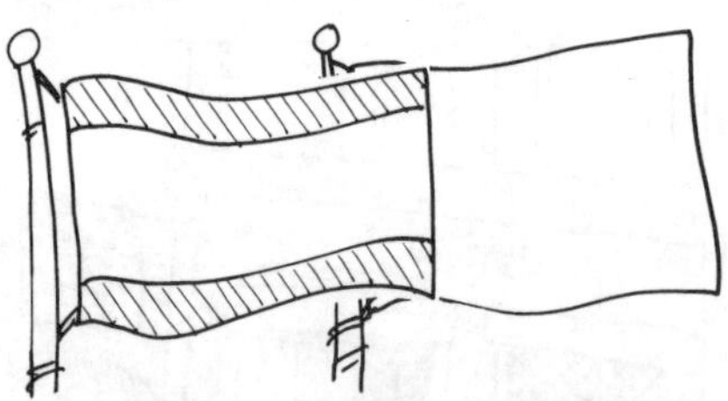

The Spanish flag is red and yellow.
What colour is your country's flag?

Colour the flags

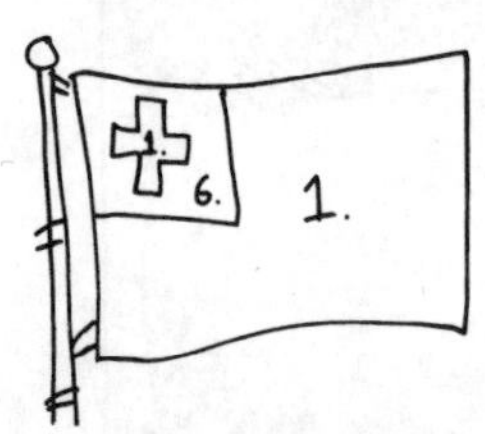

This is the Tongan flag.

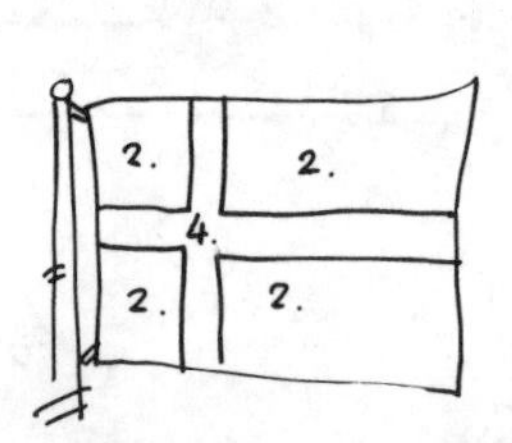

This is the Swedish flag.

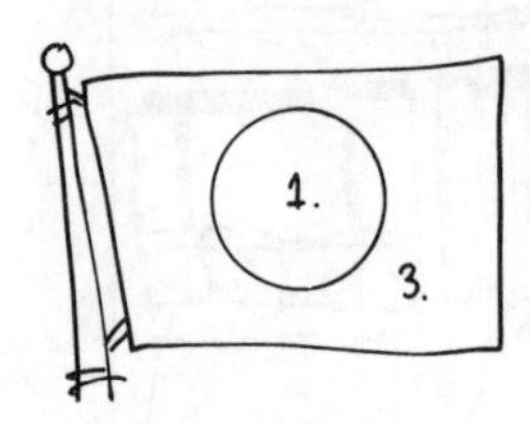

This is the Bangladeshi flag.

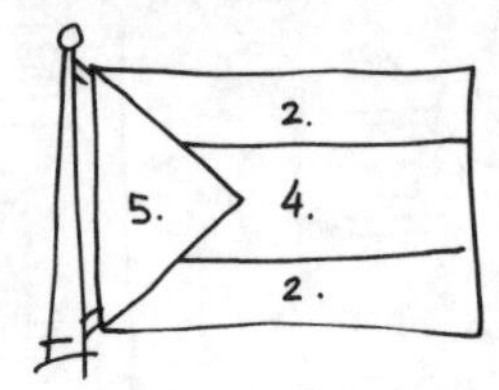

This is the Bahamian flag.

The rainbow

Prof. English Look at that rainbow!
Kit It's beautiful! Red and yellow and blue and green!
Prof. English Red, orange, yellow, green, blue, indigo and violet. Those are the colours of the spectrum.
Max Oh well, it's beautiful anyway . . . What colour is a tree, Kit?
Kit The leaves are green, but the trunk is brown.
Prof. English Right. And what colour is an orange?
Kit Orange!

leaves
trunk
leaf

Exercise

C Write short answers to the questions.
Example: 1 What colour is a cherry? *Red.*

1 What colour is a cherry?
2 What colour are your eyes?
3 And what colour are your lips?
4 What colour is an orange?
5 What colour is snow?
6 What colour is the sky on a sunny day?
7 And what colour is it on a cloudy day?
8 What colour is a leaf in spring?
9 And what colour is it in autumn?
10 What colour is a zebra?
11 What colour is a banana?

the sky
the sun
a cloud

Let's do some cooking

Kit	Let's go out.
Max	No, it's raining. Let's do some cooking!
Kit	OK.
Max	Let's make a bread and butter pudding. Where's the cook book?
Kit	Here it is, Max. We need:

6 slices of white bread
100 grams of butter
100 grams of sugar
100 grams of dried fruit
2 teaspoons of cinnamon
3 eggs
half a litre of milk

Heat your oven to 170 degrees C.
Butter a dish.
Butter the bread.
Cut the bread into small pieces.
Put a third of the bread into the bottom of the dish. Put the buttered side on top!
Put half of the dried fruit onto the bread.
Add a third of the bread. (Put the buttered side on top.)
Put half of the dried fruit onto the bread.
Add another third of the bread.
Sprinkle half of the sugar on top.
Now beat the eggs in a big bowl.
Add half of the sugar.
Sprinkle the cinnamon on the milk.
Mix the milk and the eggs.
Pour it onto the pudding.
Leave the pudding for 10 minutes.
Cook your pudding in the oven for half an hour.
Now your bread and butter pudding is ready!

Mmmm – it smells nice!
It tastes nice too!

half, quarter, third

a half   a quarter   three-quarters   a third   two-thirds

Prof. English   We say *half the bread* or *half **of** the bread.*
We say *a quarter **of**, a third **of**, two-thirds **of**, three-quarters **of** the bread.*

a (piece) of

a piece of cake   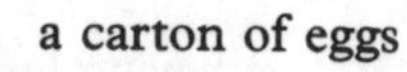a carton of eggs   a loaf of bread

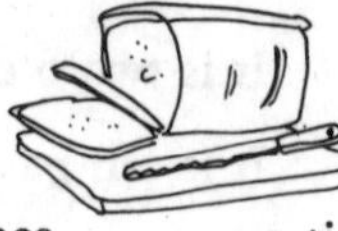

a slice of bread   a box of matches   a tin of soup

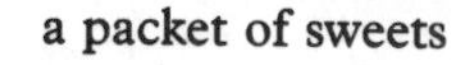a packet of sweets   a bag of flour   a piece of cheese

a bottle of milk   a jar of jam   a cup of tea/coffee

Exercise

D What are they making?

Example: 1 *Barbara is making a cheese omelette.*

cheese omelette

apple pie

cherry cake

cheese on toast

1 Barbara: 6 eggs, salt, pepper, 50 grams of butter, 100 grams of cheese
2 James and Charlie: 100 grams of cheese, 4 slices of bread, 50 grams of butter, salt, pepper
3 Brenda: 150 grams of flour, 150 grams of butter, 150 grams of sugar, 100 grams of cherries, 3 eggs, milk
4 Rosy: 200 grams of flour, 120 grams of butter, 500 grams of apples, 100 grams of sugar

11 What do you do?

Bob Brown's boring day

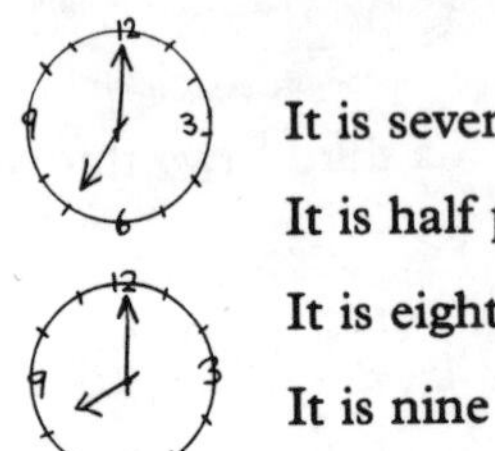

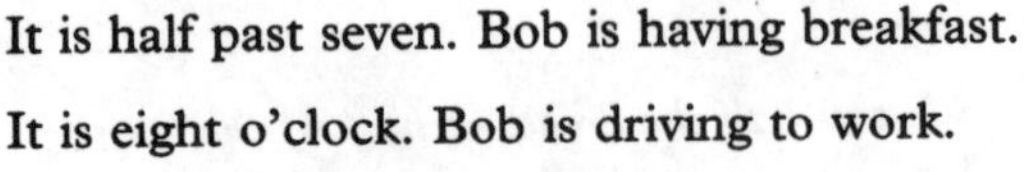

It is seven o'clock. Bob is getting up.

It is half past seven. Bob is having breakfast.

It is eight o'clock. Bob is driving to work.

It is nine o'clock. Bob is working.

It is half past ten. Bob is having a cup of coffee.

It is quarter to eleven. Bob is working again.

It is one o'clock. Bob is having lunch.

It is two o'clock. Bob is working again.

It is ten past six. Bob is driving home.

It is seven o'clock. Bob is having dinner.

It is half past seven. Bob is watching TV.

It is half past ten. Bob is having a bath.

It is eleven o'clock. Bob is having a cup of hot milk.

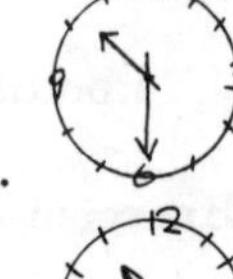

It is a quarter past eleven. Bob is reading in bed.

It is half past eleven. Bob is asleep.

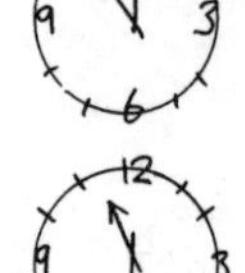

Reporter Tell us about your day, Mr Brown. What time do you get up?

Bob On Mondays, Tuesdays, Wednesdays, Thursdays and Fridays I get up at seven o'clock. I have my breakfast at half past seven. I drive to the office. I start work at nine o'clock. I have a cup of coffee at half past ten. At one o'clock I have my lunch, and I have a cup of tea at four o'clock. I finish work at half past five. I drive home.

I have dinner at seven o'clock. I watch TV. I have my bath. I have a cup of hot milk at eleven o'clock and I go to bed at a quarter past eleven.

Reporter That's very interesting, Mr Brown. What do you do on Saturdays and Sundays?

Bob I clean my car. I go shopping. I work in my garden.

Reporter But when do you make your CDs?

Bob CDs?

Reporter Yes. You're Barry Brown, the famous pop singer!

Bob No, no! I'm not a singer. Barry Brown's my brother. I'm Bob Brown.

Reporter Oh!

famous

beginning and starting
stopping and finishing

Prof. English
Sometimes **begin** and **start** are the same. *The film starts at 8 p.m.* and *The film begins at 8 p.m.* are both OK.
Bob starts work at 9 a.m. is the same as *Bob begins work at 9 a.m.*

Sometimes **finish** and **stop** are the same. You can say *Bob stops work at 5 p.m.*, or *Bob finishes work at 5 p.m.*
But we don't say *The film stops at 9.50 p.m.* And we don't talk about beginning or finishing a car. We **start** a car, and we **stop** it.

Do you . . .? Are you . . . ing?

Prof. English Do you drink coffee, Kit?

Kit No, I don't. Cats don't drink coffee. Do you drink coffee, Professor?

Prof. English Yes, I do. I drink coffee, but I'm not drinking coffee **now**. I'm talking to you!

Do you read detective stories?

I read detective stories. **I do not read** animal stories.
You read animal stories. **You do not read** adventure stories.
Tim **reads** adventure stories. **He does not read** detective stories.
Barbara **reads** animal stories, love stories and horror stories.
She does not read detective stories.
We read detective stories, science fiction and adventure stories.
We do not read love stories.
James and Charlie **read** science fiction stories, horror stories and animal stories. **They do not read** love stories or detective stories.

Reporter Charlie, what do you read?

Charlie I read science fiction stories, horror stories and animal stories.

Reporter Do you read love stories?

Charlie No, I don't. And I don't read detective stories.

Reporter What are you reading now?

Charlie *The Black Cat* by Edgar Allan Poe.

Reporter *The Black Cat*. Is that an animal story?

Charlie Well, yes. But it's a horror story too.

a horror story

a science fiction story

an animal story

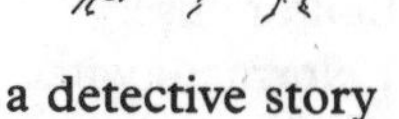
a detective story

an adventure story

a love story

Prof. English It's easy. *I, you, we, they* ***read;*** *he, she or it* ***reads.*** **Do** *I, you, we, they* ***read?*** and **Does** *he, she or it* ***read?*** Now **you** do it with *drive, swim, dance, eat, drink, run, jump, climb, sing . . .*

Max But **have** is different. *I, you, we and they* ***have;*** *he, she or it* ***has.***

Prof. English That's right. ***Has***, not *haves. I* ***have*** *my breakfast at seven o'clock in the morning, and Max* ***has*** *his at eight . . .* Where's Kit?

Max She's at home. She's having her breakfast.

Prof. English But it's eleven o'clock!

Max Kit gets up very late!

Exercise

A Put the correct words in the spaces.
Example: 1 Charlie *reads* adventure stories.

start; watch; have; drink; go; help; read; write; drive; finish

1 Charlie .... adventure stories.
2 We .... breakfast at seven o'clock.
3 The students .... lunch at 12 noon.
4 Brenda .... television on Sunday evenings.
5 My brothers .... to the cinema on Saturdays.
6 My mother .... tea at four o'clock.
7 Bob .... work at nine o'clock and .... work at five thirty.
8 Tim .... coffee in the morning.
9 Doctors .... people.
10 Barbara .... a taxi.
11 Bus drivers .... buses.
12 Authors .... books and plays.

What do you do?

Reporter Fred, what do you do?
Fred I'm a builder. I build houses.
Reporter What about you, Norman, what do you do for a living?
Norman I'm a painter.
Reporter Do you paint pictures?
Norman No, I don't. I'm not an artist! I paint houses. Fred builds them, and I paint them.

build

(sing) + er
Liza Minelli is a singer.
Diego Maradona is a footballer.
Professor English is a teacher.
David Hockney is a painter. He paints pictures.
Norman is a painter too. He paints houses.

(dance) + r
Darcy Bussell is a dancer.
Rosy Border is a writer.
Barbara Williams is a driver.

(swim) + mer
Adrian Moorhouse is a swimmer.
Linford Christie is a runner.

Prof. English This man's cooking. He's a **cook**. And that's a **cooker**.

Reporter And now I'm talking to Will Shakespeare in London . . . Will, what do you do for a living?

Will I'm a writer.

Reporter What do you write?

Will Plays. I'm writing a play now.

Reporter That's very interesting. What's it called?

Will *Romeo and Juliet*. It's a love story.

Prof. English We say *What do you do for a living?* or *What do you do?*

Exercises

B Answer the questions.

Example: 1 *I get up at 7 a.m.*

1 What time do you get up in the morning?
2 What time do you go to bed at night?
3 Do you drink coffee?
4 What do you do for a living?
5 Do you read love stories?
6 What are you reading now?
7 Do you read in bed?
8 Do you listen to pop music?
9 Do you sing in the bath?
10 Do you eat sweets?

C Write sentences.

Example: 1 *I'm a driver.*

1	drive	6	write
2	play football	7	sing
3	paint	8	dance
4	build	9	jump
5	run	10	teach

12 Always interesting

dirty and clean, noisy and quiet

a dirty car

a clean car

a noisy car

a quiet car

Prof. English *Dirty* and *clean* are **adjectives**.
An adjective tells us about a
noun . . . Kit, you're very noisy
– please be quiet!

Kit Sorry. I'm quiet now. OK?

Prof. English We talk about **opposites**.
The opposite of *wet* is *dry*.
The opposite of *early* is *late*.
The opposite of *good* is *bad*.
The opposite of *nice* is *nasty*.
The opposite of *interesting* is *boring*.
How many pairs of opposites can you find?

Exercise

A What are the opposites of these?

Example: 1 *The opposite of a cold day is a hot day.*

1 a cold day
2 dry shoes
3 a small cat
4 a short man
5 a short skirt
6 a long queue of people
7 a beautiful animal
8 an interesting story
9 a thin cat
10 a cloudy day
11 long trousers
12 a fat person
13 new clothes
15 a good apple

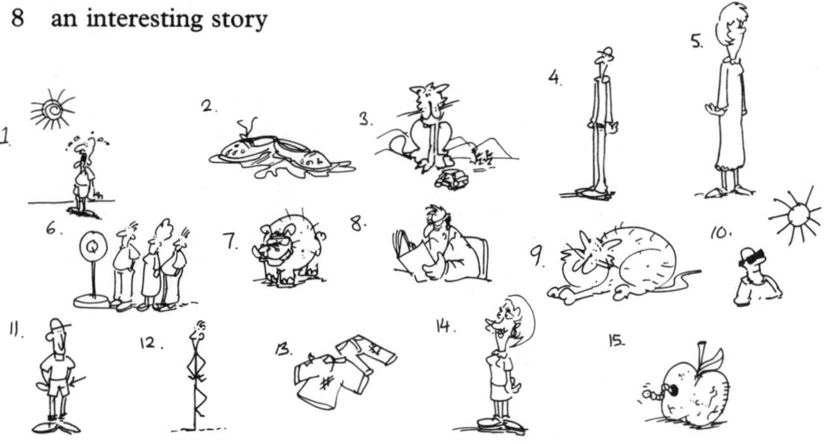

Let's eat!

Prof. English We talk about **eating** and **drinking**, but we **have** meals. *Breakfast, lunch, tea, dinner* and *supper* are all *meals*. And we sometimes have a *snack* between meals! What time do you have breakfast, Kit? And what time do you have lunch?

Kit I don't have breakfast, and I don't have lunch. I get up at eleven o'clock and I have brunch!

What do you have for breakfast?

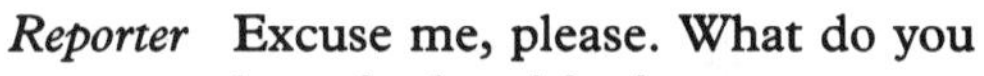

Reporter Excuse me, please. What do you have for breakfast?

Man Two eggs, a slice of toast and a cup of coffee.

Reporter Thank you . . . Excuse me, what do you have for breakfast?

Woman I have a glass of orange juice, two slices of bread and two cups of nice, hot tea.

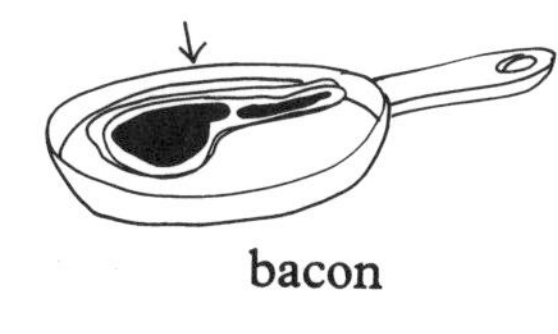

bacon

Reporter And what do you have for breakfast?

Boy Bacon, tomatoes, toast and tea.

Reporter And who cooks your breakfast?

Boy My mother.

Reporter Excuse me, what do you have for breakfast?

Girl I don't eat breakfast. I have a snack at ten o'clock.

Prof. English

Some people have lunch in the middle of the day and dinner in the evening. Some people have dinner in the middle of the day and tea or supper in the evening.

On weekdays I have dinner in the evening, but on Sundays I have my dinner in the middle of the day. And on Sundays I have tea and cakes in the afternoon. I have supper in the evening.

always, usually, often, sometimes, never

It is **always** cold in Antarctica.

It is **sometimes** foggy in England.

It is **nearly always** dry in the Sahara Desert.

It is **usually** hot in India.

It is **often** windy in Scotland.

It is **hardly ever** cold in Tenerife.

It is **never** snowy in Arizona.

Prof. English *Always, usually, sometimes* and *never* are **adverbs**. An adverb says something about a verb. Max, what time do you get up?

Max I **usually** get up at about eight. But **sometimes** I get up at seven. I **hardly ever** get up at six.

Kit I **rarely** get up early.

Prof. English **Rarely** is like **hardly ever** . . . I am rarely boring.

Max Well . . . you are sometimes boring, Professor.

Prof. English Oh dear!

nearly and almost

Tim Barbara, are you ready?

Barbara I'm nearly ready. I'm putting my lipstick on.

Barbara is not ready, but she is almost ready.

Prof. English **Nearly** is like **almost**. But we don't say *nearly never.*

Kit Why not?

Prof. English I don't know!

Exercise

B Put a tick (√) or a cross (×) in the spaces.

Example: 1 It is often sunny in Spain. (√)

1 It is often sunny in Spain. ( )
2 The weather in Antarctica is sometimes hot. ( )
3 It is always cold and windy in England. ( )
4 In France, women often wear lipstick. ( )
5 The weather in Arizona is usually hot and dry. ( )
6 Professor English is never boring. ( )
7 Barbara rarely has a shower in the morning. ( )
8 It hardly ever rains in Scotland. ( )
9 Kit nearly always gets up very late. ( )
10 Max always gets up at six o'clock in the morning. ( )

How often?

Reporter	How often do you go to London, madam?
1st woman	Oh, about five times a month.
Reporter	What do you do there?
1st woman	I usually go shopping, or sometimes I go to a concert.
Reporter	Thank you . . . Excuse me, madam, how often do you go to London?
2nd woman	Never! I never go to London.
Reporter	Why not?
2nd woman	It's dirty and noisy. It smells.
Reporter	Thank you . . . Sir, how often do you go to London?
Man	Five times a week. I work there.
Reporter	How do you get there?
Man	I usually go by train. But sometimes I drive.

Prof. English	You can go to work by train, by car, by taxi, by bus, or by boat, by air, by helicopter . . .
Kit	I walk to work.
Prof. English	Ah, you go on foot.
Kit	Why don't we say *on feet*? People have two feet, and cats have four . . .

I (have a bath)
once a day/every day
once a week/every week
once a month/every month
once a year/every year
twice a week
three times a month
ten times a year
every three years

Exercises

C Answer the questions.
Example: 1 *I always have toast and coffee.*

1. What do you have for breakfast? (always toast and coffee)
2. What do you read in the evenings? (usually horror stories)
3. What time do you have lunch? (nearly always 1 p.m.)
4. Do you wear shoes? (nearly always)
5. Do you wear a hat? (hardly ever)
6. Do you sing in the shower? (often)
7. Do you go to work by taxi? (hardly ever)
8. Do you take an umbrella to work? (hardly ever)
9. Do you listen to opera? (sometimes)
10. Do you wear lipstick? (never)
11. Do you have a snack in the middle of the afternoon? (sometimes)
12. Do you drink champagne? (never)

D Answer the questions. Use *once a day, nearly every day, once a week, twice a week, once a month, once a year, hardly ever,* etc.
Example: 1 How often do you have a shower? *Once a day.*

1. How often do you have a shower?
2. How often do you take a taxi?
3. How often do you go shopping?
4. How often do you wash your ears?
5. How often do you buy a book?
6. How often do you go to the cinema?
7. How often do you clean your room?
8. How often do you buy flowers?
9. How often do you have dinner in a restaurant?
10. How often do you read love stories?

13 Work and hobbies

Where do you live?
Where do you work?

Prof. English What do you do for a living, Rosy?

Rosy I'm a writer.

Prof. English Where do you live?

Rosy I live with my husband in Suffolk. That's in the east of England.

Prof. English Where do you work?

Rosy I usually work at home. I have an office upstairs. I take my little dog for a walk, then I sit down at my desk and I work for seven or eight hours. The dog sits under my desk. She's very quiet and good.

Prof. English What do you do in the evenings?

Rosy I usually cook dinner for my husband. Sometimes our son visits us. He is 21 and he's always hungry. We have dinner and then we talk or read or listen to music. Sometimes we play Scrabble. It's a word game.

Prof. English I often play Scrabble. It's a very nice game. Do you play chess too?

Rosy Not very often. It's a difficult game, and I'm often too tired in the evening.

Where does the Queen live?

Reporter Where does the Queen live?
Boy Buckingham Palace. That's in London. She works there too. She has an office there. Her dogs sit under her desk.
Girl But she has another house called Windsor Castle. That's near London.
Reporter Where does the Queen go for her holidays?
Girl She usually goes to Sandringham for her winter holidays.
Reporter Sandringham? Where's that? Do you know?
Boy It's in the east of England. The Queen has another very big house there.
Reporter Where does she go for her summer holidays?
Girl Balmoral Castle. That's another big house. Balmoral is in Scotland. She usually goes there by air. Her dogs go with her.

Reporter Colin Cameron is a window-cleaner. Tell us about your work, Colin.
Colin Well, I clean windows. I fill my bucket with water. I climb my ladder. I wash the windows with a wet cloth. I polish them with a dry cloth . . .
Reporter Do you ever fall off your ladder?
Colin Hardly ever. I'm always careful. I'm never careless.
Reporter Do you ever look through the windows?
Colin Sometimes. But not very often.

with

Prof. English	I always eat **with** a knife and fork. Chinese people always eat **with** chopsticks.
Kit	They don't eat soup with chopsticks! They eat soup with a spoon.
Prof. English	OK, OK. I eat soup with a spoon too . . . I write letters **with** a pen. Colin washes the windows **with** a wet cloth . . . Kit, what are you doing?
Kit	I'm polishing my shoes.
Prof. English	But you're polishing them with my handkerchief! Go and get an old cloth, please.

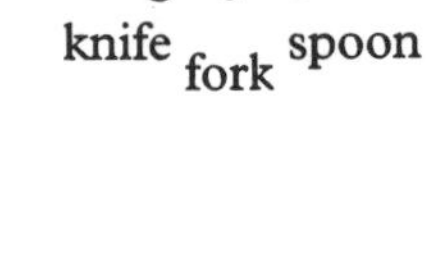

knife fork spoon

chopsticks

Hobbies

Prof. English
Hobbies are things that we do in our **free time** – when we aren't working. My hobbies are gardening and playing chess. What do you do in your free time? Do you swim? Do you go shopping? Do you dance, or play football, or go to concerts?

Tim	What's your hobby, Charlie?
Charlie	Playing football. I play football every Saturday. I'm in the school football team.
Tim	Super! Do you often win?
Charlie	Yes, we do. We nearly always win; we hardly ever lose.

Exercise

A Look at the pictures and write the conversations.

Example: 	*Reporter:* *What's your hobby?*
Me: *My hobby is gardening.*
Reporter: *How often do you garden?*
Me: *I garden every day.*

1 gardening
2
3
4
5
6 playing computer games
7 going fishing
8
9 going to the cinema
10 going to the pub
11 going to parties
12
13
14

fast

Harry is a **good** driver. He has a **fast** car, and he drives it **fast**. But he nearly always drives **well**. He hardly ever drives **badly**. He is a **careful** driver. He nearly always drives **carefully**. He hardly ever drives **carelessly**.

Prof. English — *Fast, well, badly* and *carefully* are **adverbs**. They tell you about a verb. Noisy people talk noisily. Quiet people talk quietly. Dangerous drivers drive dangerously. I am an interesting teacher. I teach English very interestingly.

Max — I always listen to you very politely, because I am a polite person. But look at Kit – she's asleep!

polite

Prof. English
How do you make an adverb? Usually you add **ly** to an adjective:
careful + ly (and careless + ly)
slow + ly (and quick + ly)
interesting + ly
beautiful + ly
sad + ly
nice + ly
. . . and usual + ly

When the adjective ends in **e,** you take off the **e** and add **ly**:
terrible – terribly

When the adjective ends in **y,** you take off the **y** and add **ily**:
noisy – noisily
nasty – nastily

James sings noisily.

"You smell!" says Barbara nastily.

But the adverb of *good* is **well,** and the adverb of *fast* is **fast**. I have a *fast* car. (We never say *a quick car.*)

fast

buying and selling

Brenda is buying Amy an ice cream.

Prof. English	We say *Brenda is buying an ice cream* **for** *Amy* or *Brenda is buying Amy an ice cream.* We say *Bill is selling a bike* **to** *James* or *Bill is selling James a bike.*
Max	A *bike* is a bicycle.
Kit	A *cycle* is a bicycle too.

Bill is selling James a bicycle.

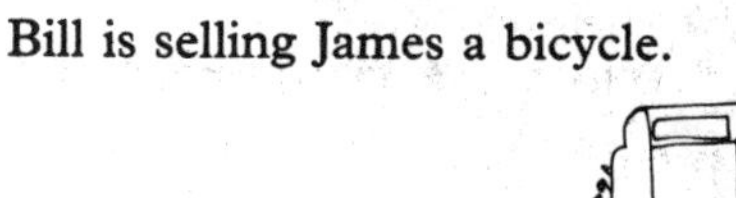

Money

Prof. English	We buy things with *money.*
	These are *coins.*
	This is a *penny.* These are *pence.*
	This is a *two pence piece.*
	This is a *five pence piece.*
	This is a *ten pence piece.*
	This is a *twenty pence piece.*
	This is a *fifty pence piece.*
	This is a *pound.* There are 100 pence in a pound.
	This is a *two pound coin.*
	These are *notes.*
	This is a *five pound note.*
Max	Look – a fiver!
	This is a *ten pound note.*
Kit	A tenner!
Prof. English	This is a *twenty pound note.*
	This is a *fifty pound note.*

How much is it?
How much does it cost?

Prof. English — We buy things or pay for things with money. (**Pay for** is like *buy*.) We say *How much does it cost?* or *How much is it?* And the answer is the **price** . . . Max, how much does a litre of milk cost?

Max — I don't know. I never buy milk. Ask Kit. She drinks milk every day . . . Kit, how much is a litre of milk?

Kit — About sixty pence.

Prof. English — You can say *about sixty pence* or *approximately sixty pence*. This stamp costs twenty-six *pence*.

Max — We sometimes say *p* (for *penny*): a stamp costs 26p.

Prof. English — OK. There are a hundred pence – or 100p – in a pound. How many pence are there in £2.87? in £13.84? in £156.40? in £3,426.97?

Kit — Stop, stop! I haven't got a calculator!

cheap and expensive

Prof. English — We say ***high*** *prices* and ***low*** *prices*, and ***expensive*** *things* and ***cheap*** *things*. £129,999 is a high price for a car . . .

Max — Wow! That's an expensive car!

Prof. English — £129.99 is a low price for a car . . .

Kit — Wow! That's a cheap car!

Exercises

B Make adverbs!

Example: 1 Pavarotti sings *beautifully.*

1 Pavarotti sings (beautiful).
2 The old woman walks very (slow).
3 Barbara drives very (fast).
4 Charlie plays his CDs very (noisy).
5 Brenda usually talks (quiet).
6 I eat my breakfast (quick).
7 Barbara cooks very (good).
8 Amy paints very (nice).

C Put pronouns in the spaces.

Example: 1 Tim sometimes buys Barbara flowers.
He sometimes buys *her* flowers.

1 Tim sometimes buys Barbara flowers.
.... sometimes buys .... flowers.
2 Bill is selling James a bike.
.... is selling .... a bike.
3 Harry's mother often sends the Williams children presents.
.... often sends .... presents.
4 Charlie is giving Brenda a kiss.
.... is giving .... a kiss.
5 Harry often buys the children sweets.
.... often buys .... sweets.
6 The man in the cake shop is selling Brenda and Harry a cake.
.... is selling .... a cake.

D Ask for these things, pay for them and get your change.

Example: 1

Me: *I'd like a toothbrush, please.*
Shopkeeper: *What colour would you like?*
Me: *Green, please.*
Shopkeeper: *Here you are. That's eighty-nine pence, please.*
Me: *Here's a pound.*
Shopkeeper: *And here's eleven pence change. Thank you very much.*

a toothbrush

1 a green toothbrush – 89p (£1)
2 a red T-shirt – £7.95 (£10)
3 a pair of black and white socks – £2.25 (£3)
4 a purple hat – £12.50 (£20)
5 a brown bag – £24.99 (£25)
6 six red and yellow plates – £12.30 (£15)

14 The biggest and the best

Two jumpers

Barbara I need a new jumper. Let's go shopping.

Tim OK.

Barbara sees a jumper in a shop window.

Barbara Look at that beautiful jumper, Tim. How much does it cost?

Tim I don't know. It's very nice, but it looks expensive – and there isn't a price ticket on it.

Barbara Let's go inside and ask.

Shop assistant Hello, can I help you?

Barbara How much is that jumper in the window?

The shop assistant looks at the jumper. There is a very small price ticket inside it.

Shop assistant Eighty-nine pounds ninety-nine pence.

Tim *(very quietly)* That's nearly ninety pounds, Barbara.

Barbara Yes. It's very expensive.

They go outside. There are some big notices outside a church hall.

Tim Oh, look, Barbara – a jumble sale! My mother sometimes buys the children's clothes in jumble sales. People give their nearly-new clothes. The helpers sell the clothes very cheaply and give the money to poor people. Let's go in.

Woman It costs 50p to go in, please.

Tim OK, here's £1. Come on, Barbara.

Girl helper It's hot in here!

Woman helper Take your jumper off, my dear.

The girl takes her jumper off and puts it on the table.

Tim sees the jumper.

Tim Look at that jumper, Barbara!

Barbara Oh, yes! Thank you, Tim. *(She looks at it carefully.)* This is a very nice jumper. It's nearly new too . . . Excuse me, how much is this jumper?

Woman helper Oh . . . 75p.

Barbara 75p? That's very cheap! Hold my bag, please, Tim. *(She puts on the jumper.)* Do I look OK?

Tim You look beautiful. It's a super jumper. *(to the woman)* Here's a fiver.

Girl helper Hey, excuse me! That's my new jumper!

Barbara Sorry!

Tim Sorry!

Jumble sales and car boot sales

Reporter Excuse me, why do you go to jumble sales? Is it because you're poor?

Woman No, it's because the clothes are very good and very cheap. I have three children. They grow very quickly. They need new clothes every few months. I go to car boot sales too.

Reporter Car boot sales? Do they sell boots?

Woman No . . . well, yes, they sometimes sell boots. People bring things in their car boots. They park the cars in a big field. Then they sell their old clothes, books, CDs, plates and cups . . . Boot sales are very interesting.

Kit	Good morning. A litre of milk, please.
Shopkeeper	62p, please.
Kit	Here's £1.
Shopkeeper	And here's 38p change. Thank you very much.

Exercise

A Now you! Write the conversations:

1 a carton of 12 eggs – £1.20 (£2)
2 a jar of jam – 72p (£1)
3 a packet of butter – 80p (£1)
4 500 grams of cheese – £2.25 (£2.50)
5 a bottle of champagne – £22 (£25)
6 a loaf of bread – 43p (50p)
7 a kilo of tomatoes – 92p (£1)
8 500 grams of cherries – £1.20 (£5)

more expensive

	Britain	France	USA	Japan
Cinema ticket	£8.00	£5.75	£5.50	£12.00
Chicken	£3.50	£7.00	£3.50	£8.50
Ice cream	80p	90p	60p	£1.20
Pair of shoes	£65.00	£110.00	£125.00	£200.00
Bottle of wine	£4.99	£3.49	£7.00	£8.00
Toothbrush	£1.15	£1.25	99p	£2.00
1 litre of petrol	56p	83p	24p	64p
1 litre of milk	60p	£1.00	65p	£1.50

A litre of milk is **more expensive** in Japan **than** it is in the USA.
A cinema ticket is **cheaper** in Britain **than** it is in Japan.
A bottle of wine is **more expensive** in the USA **than** it is in France.
A litre of petrol is **cheaper** in the USA **than** it is in Japan.
A chicken is **more expensive** in Japan **than** it is in France.
An ice cream is **cheaper** in Britain **than** it is in Japan.

Exercise

B Now you! Write about a toothbrush and a pair of shoes; then write about prices in your country.

Comparatives

Prof. English — I'm talking about **comparatives**. *Cheaper* is the comparative of *cheap*. *More expensive* is the comparative of *expensive*. Short adjectives usually add **er**.

Max — *Cheaper, older, longer, shorter, quicker, faster.*

Kit — But we don't say *gooder*, we say ***better***. Why?

Prof. English — Don't ask difficult questions! Adjectives like *big, fat, thin, sad* add **ger, ter, ner, der** – *bigger, fatter, thinner, sadder*. But we don't say *badder*; we say ***worse***. And adjectives with **e** at the end add **r**.

Max — Like *nicer*.

Prof. English — That's right. And words with **y** . . .

Max — Don't tell us – you take off the **y** and add **ier**.

Kit — Like *noisier, nastier, easier, smellier, sillier.*

Prof. English — That's right. And long adjectives usually take **more**.

Kit — *More expensive, more difficult, more beautiful, more interesting.*

Max — More boring too. Come on, Kit! Let's play football! It's more interesting than the Professor's lessons.

bigger than, not as big as

Charlie is **older than** Amy, but he is **not as old as** Barbara.
Barbara is **bigger than** Amy, and bigger than Charlie,
but she is **not as big as** James.
Is Amy **as big as** Charlie? No, she is not.
Is Charlie **as old as** James? No, he is not.
Charlie is three years younger than James.

Barbara and Tim are reading the newspaper.

Barbara Look, Tim: "Film Star's Careless Driving" . . . There's a picture of her here. Am I as beautiful as her, Tim?

Tim . . . Er, no, Barbara. But you're a better driver!

Lady Bracknell Some people say *as beautiful as her*, or *better than them*, or *taller than me*. They are wrong! It's really **as beautiful as she, better than they** and **taller than I**.

Prof. English Yes, I know, but it sounds very old-fashioned. I always say and write *as beautiful as she is*, and *taller than I am*. It's correct, and it doesn't sound old-fashioned.

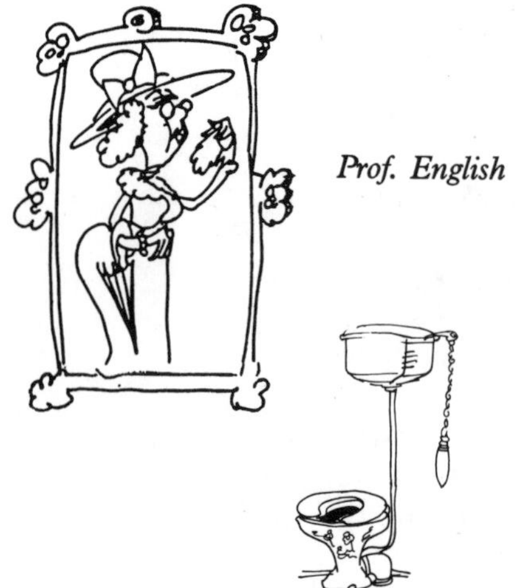

It looks old-fashioned.

It sounds old-fashioned.

Exercise

C Look at this picture and write questions and answers.

Examples: *Is Ted as old as Laura? No, he is not.*
Is Laura taller than Ben? Yes, she is.

ill and well

Kit	How are you, Professor?
Prof. English	I'm very well, thank you. I'm hardly ever ill. How are you, and how's Max?
Kit	I'm fine, but Max isn't well.
Prof. English	Poor Max! He's ill. English people say *ill*. Americans say *sick*.
Kit	But English people sometimes say *sick* too, Professor. I'm always sick in boats.
Prof. English	Ah, you're *seasick*. People can be *seasick*, *carsick* and *airsick* too. And the comparative of *ill* is ***worse***.
Kit	Stop talking about it! I feel sick now!

ill

sick

rich and poor

Prof. English	**Poor** is the opposite of **rich**.
Kit	I'm poor. I've only got 20p.
Prof. English	But we also say ***Poor** Max* – he's ill.
	Kit telephones Max.
Kit	Hello, Max. How are you? Are you better?
Max	No, I'm worse. I feel terrible. I'm in bed.
Kit	Poor Max. Get well soon!

tall, taller, tallest

Amy is not very tall. Charlie is **taller** than Amy.
Who is the **tallest**? James is.
Who is the **oldest**? Barbara is.
Who has the **biggest** feet? James has.
Who is the **youngest**? Amy is.

Prof. English *Biggest, tallest, most beautiful* are superlatives.

Adjective	Comparative	Superlative
old	old**er**	old**est**
nice	nice**r**	nice**st**
big	big**ger**	big**gest**
beautiful	**more** beautiful	**most** beautiful
good	better	best
bad	worse	worst

Prof. English Here are a few interesting superlatives.

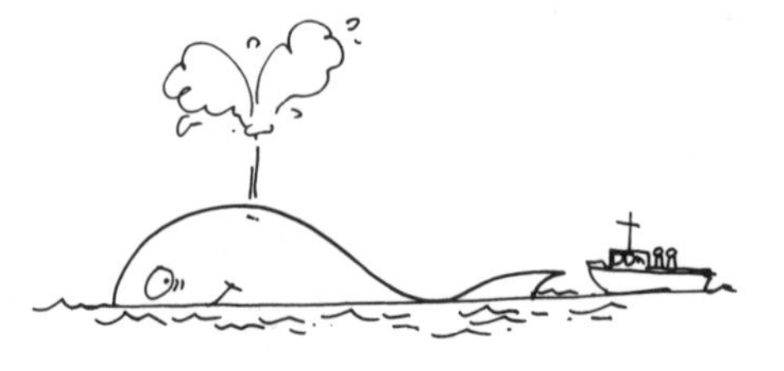

The biggest animal in the world is the blue whale.
Some blue whales are 30 metres long.
The biggest tree in the world is called General Sherman, and it is in the USA. General Sherman is 83 metres 30 centimetres tall and nearly three thousand years old.

Prof. English ***I am called*** *English* is like ***My name is*** *English.*

General Sherman is very tall, but it is not the tallest tree in the world. The tallest tree in the world is 113 metres tall, but its trunk is not as fat as General Sherman's.

The tallest office building in the world is the Sears Tower. It is in Chicago in the USA. It is 4,775 metres high. It has 16,000 windows. 16,700 people work inside it.
The biggest swimming pool in the world is in Morocco, and it is 480 metres long and 75 metres wide.

The longest car in the world is nearly 22 metres long. It has a TV, a swimming pool, telephones and seats for 20 people.

15 What do you want?

can and can't

Prof. English We write **cannot**. We say **can't**.

Barbara and Tim are at the cinema. They are watching an exciting film, but a woman in front of them is wearing a hat. Barbara cannot see the screen.

Tim Are you OK, Barbara?

Barbara No, I'm not. There's a lady in front of me. She's wearing a big hat and I can't see the screen . . . Excuse me, please take your hat off. I can't see the film.

Woman Sorry. Can you see the film now?

Barbara Yes, I can. Thank you.

A man behind them is eating crisps very noisily.

Tim Please be quiet. We can't hear the film!

Man Sorry, I can't hear you . . . Would you like a crisp?

the screen

can and may

Amy Can I play tennis this afternoon, please?

Brenda No, you can't. You're going to the dentist.

Prof. English Amy **can** play tennis. She is a good tennis player. But this afternoon her mother is taking her to the dentist. The correct word here is **may**: *May I play tennis?* But we often say **can**. It's OK.

Child May I play with your little dog, please?

Lady Bracknell No, you may not.

Child Why not?

Lady Bracknell Because my dog bites children!

too big, not big enough

Prof. English Why can't Barbara wear that dress?

Kit Because it's too small.

Max Because she isn't thin enough.

Prof. English Why can't Amy get those biscuits?

Kit Because the shelf is too high.

Max Because she isn't tall enough.

biscuits

I like cats!

Tim likes Barbara. Does Tim like Barbara? Yes, he does.

Brenda likes dogs, and dogs usually like her. Does Brenda like dogs? Yes, she does. Do dogs like her? Yes, they do.

Harry does not like noisy music. Does Harry like noisy music? No, he does not.

Barbara does not like tomatoes. Does Barbara like tomatoes? No, she does not.

Charlie likes flowers, because they are beautiful and because they smell nice.

I like skiing!

James likes skiing.
Mr Duncan likes playing his double bass.

Charlie does not like cleaning his shoes.
Amy does not like going to the dentist.

Write	**Say**
I/you/we/they do not like he/she/it does not like 	I/you/we/they don't like he/she/it doesn't like 

Reporter	Good morning. Today we're talking about animals. Excuse me, sir, do you like cats?
Man	Yes, I do.
Reporter	Why do you like cats?
Man	Cats are quiet and clean.
Reporter	And do you like dogs?
Man	No, I don't. Dogs are too noisy and dirty. They're smelly too.
Reporter	Thank you. Excuse me, madam, have you got a cat?
Woman	No, I haven't. I don't like cats.
Reporter	Why don't you like cats?
Woman	Because they chase birds.

Prof. English	I **like** coffee, and I **like** reading. Kit, do you like playing the fiddle?
Kit	Yes, I do. I **love** playing the fiddle.
Prof. English	And do you like swimming?
Kit	No, I don't.
Prof. English	There! Kit **dislikes** swimming.
Kit	No, I don't. I **hate** swimming!

love like dislike hate

Exercise

A Let's talk about likes and dislikes. Read the words and put a tick (√) in the box for "like" and a cross (×) for "dislike".

Cats	☐	Short skirts	☐
Dogs	☐	Fast cars	☐
Mice	☐	Flowers	☐
Coffee	☐	Pop music	☐
Horror stories	☐	Football	☐
Going to the cinema	☐	Bread and butter pudding	☐
Going to concerts	☐	Animal stories	☐
Cucumbers	☐		

Fred and Jimmy

Fred is going on holiday, but he cannot take his dog. Fred's dog is called Jimmy, and Fred loves him very much.

Fred Hello, is that Hammond's Happy Holiday Home for Dogs?

Hammond Yes, it is. I'm Horace Hammond. Can I help you?

Fred Yes. Please tell me about your happy holiday home for dogs.

Hammond Well, the dogs have a long walk every day.

Fred Oh dear, Jimmy dislikes long walks. He's too old and fat, and his legs are too short . . . What do the dogs have for breakfast?

Hammond They usually have dog biscuits.

Fred Jimmy hates dog biscuits. They aren't soft enough for him . . . Where do the dogs sleep?

Hammond They usually sleep in a kennel in the garden.

Fred Jimmy hates sleeping in a kennel. It isn't warm enough for him. He doesn't like sleeping outside. He likes sleeping in the house. He always sleeps on my bed.

Hammond Well, a few very old, ill dogs sleep in the house. But they never sleep on my bed!

hard

soft

want

Tim	Barbara, you don't **need** those shoes. You've got 24 pairs of shoes and 11 pairs of boots at home.
Barbara	But I **want** them! They're pretty, and they aren't very expensive, and I love new shoes!

Prof. English	I **want** an ice cream. I don't **need** an ice cream, because I'm not hungry. But I **want** an ice cream. I **don't want** a biscuit or an éclair. I **want** an ice cream. Do you want an ice cream, Kit?
Kit	No, thank you, I don't.
Prof. English	Well, **what do you want**?
Kit	A bottle of milk. I'm thirsty.

Write and say

I/you/we/they **want**
he/she/it **wants**

Write 

I/you/we/they **do not want**
he/she/it **does not want**

Say 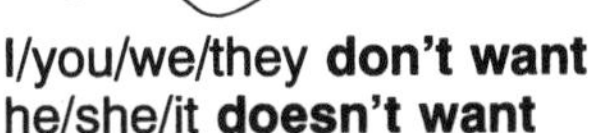

I/you/we/they **don't want**
he/she/it **doesn't want**

Exercise

B What do you want?

Example: 1 *I want an ice cream.*

1 2 3 4 5 6

want + noun
want to + verb

Prof. English We say *I **want** an ice cream* and *I **want** a pair of shoes,* and we say *I **want to** have a shower, I **want to** go to London.* We don't say *I want to an ice cream,* or *I want go to London . . .*
Kit, do you want to go to the concert with me?

Kit No, thank you, Professor. I'm too tired. I want to go to bed.

Prof. English What about you, Max?

Max No, thank you. I don't want to listen to music. I want to go to a disco. I love dancing.

a disco

Tim Hello, Barbara's Taxis.

Mr Duncan Hello, Duncan here; may I speak to Barbara, please?

Tim Barbara, it's Mr Duncan.

Barbara I'm in the bathroom. What does he want?

Tim He wants a taxi.

Barbara Yes, of course. But where does he want to go? And what time does he want to leave home?

Tim Hello, Mr Duncan. Where do you want to go, please, and what time do you want to leave home?

Mr Duncan I want to go to the railway station, and I want to leave home at half past five in the morning, please. Is that too early? My train leaves at a quarter past six.

Tim He wants to leave home at half past five in the morning, and he wants to go to the railway station.

Barbara OK, fine.

Exercises

C What do they need?

Example: 1 *The car needs a wheel.*

D What do they want to do?

Example: *Barbara doesn't want to clean the car. She wants to go shopping.*

Barbara: clean the car (×), go shopping (√)
Tim: watch TV (×), write letters (√)
Amy: go to the dentist (×), play tennis (√)
Harry: mend Charlie's bicycle (×), work in the garden (√)
Brenda: go to London (×), go to Paris (√)
James: play chess (×), listen to music (√)

I want and I'd like

Small child I want another biscuit!
Mother Don't say "I want". Say "I'd like another biscuit, please."
Small child OK. I'd like another biscuit, please – and I want it now!

Prof. English We say *I'd like*. We write *I would like*.
Lady Bracknell *I should like* is better.
Prof. English Yes, but it sounds old-fashioned. *I would like* is OK. Would you like a biscuit?
Lady Bracknell No, thank you. I never eat biscuits. But my little dog loves biscuits!

16 I'd love one!

A weekend in Paris

alone together

Tim Good morning. I'd like to go to Paris, please.

Travel agent Certainly, sir. Do you want to go alone?

Tim No, no. My girlfriend and I want to go together.

Travel agent How do you want to travel?

Tim I don't know.

Travel agent Well, you can travel by air. It's quick, but it isn't very cheap. Or would you like to travel by train? The Eurostar train is very fast. It leaves London at 7.23. It goes through the Channel Tunnel and it arrives in Paris at 11.23. Or you can travel by bus – it isn't as expensive as the train, but it's slower, of course. Or you can take the car ferry from Dover or Ramsgate or Newhaven. Or you can drive onto a special train and go through the Channel Tunnel . . .

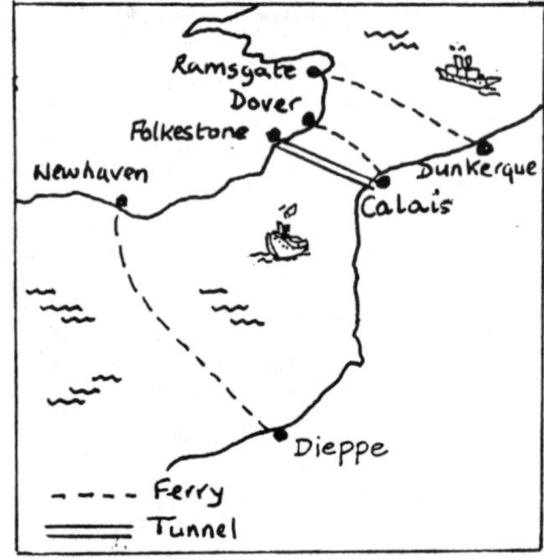

Tim Which is the cheapest?

Travel agent Well, car ferries are very cheap in winter, but in summer they are very expensive. What about a short holiday in Paris? Look at this brochure. A weekend in Paris! You travel by bus and you spend two nights in a hotel.

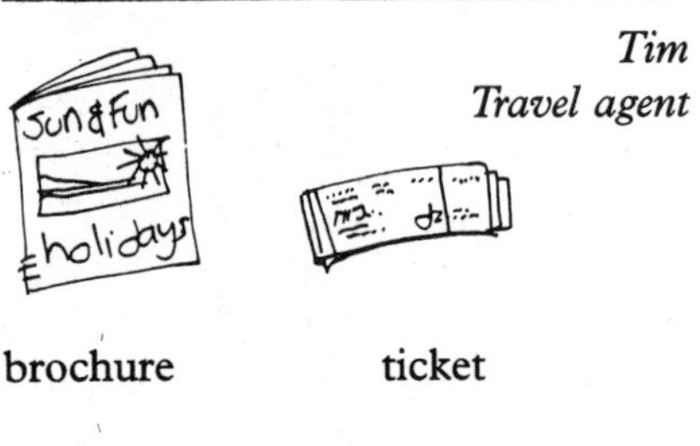

brochure ticket

Tim Super! How much does it cost?

Travel agent Two hundred and forty pounds for two people.

Tim That's fine. I'd like two tickets, please. Does the bus go on the car ferry or through the Channel Tunnel?

Travel agent It goes through the tunnel.

Tim Good. I don't like boats – I'm always seasick!

travel agent

leave, depart and arrive

Prof. English **Leave** means *go away from*. In Britain, children **leave** school at the age of 16, 17 or 18. Brenda sometimes wants to **leave** Harry.

untidy

tidy

Brenda I'm leaving you, Harry!
Harry Why?
Brenda Because you're too untidy. I'm always tidy, but you always leave your clothes on the floor.

Prof. English People usually **leave**. Trains and buses, boats and aeroplanes **leave**, or **depart from**. You can say *The bus* ***leaves*** *London at 2 o'clock* or *The bus* ***departs from*** *London at 2 o'clock.*

Arrive means *come to.* Trains and aeroplanes arrive **at** the station or **at** the airport. But we say *The train arrives* ***in*** *London at 7.10 a.m.*

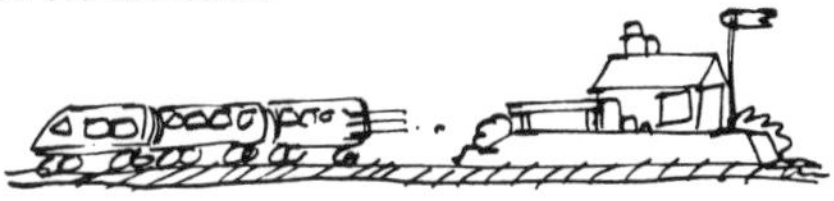

along, through, over

The car goes **along** the road and **over** the bridge.
The train goes **through** the tunnel.

spend

Prof. English We **spend** money, and we **spend** time. I often spend an hour or two in the pub. I sometimes spend £1 on a packet of biscuits. I sometimes spend a night in a hotel. What do you spend your money on?

left, right, middle

Prof. English This is my left hand, and this is my right hand. Kit is standing on my right hand side.

Kit That's right. I'm standing on your right.

Prof. English Max is standing on my left hand side.

Max Yes, I'm standing on your left.

Prof. English That's right.

Max No, left.

Prof. English OK, OK: **right** means *correct, not wrong* – and it means *not left*, too.

Max Right!

Prof. English And I'm between Kit and Max. I'm **in the middle**.

Kit Look out! You're in the middle of the road!

NO RIGHT TURN KEEP LEFT

right and wrong

This sum is right. It is correct. This sum is wrong. It is incorrect.

Tim Excuse me, I want to get to Sherman House. Where is it, please?

Man It's in the middle of the town. Turn right here. Go along the road for about 200 metres. Then turn left at the traffic lights. Go straight on for about 300 metres. Sherman House is a big office building on the left hand side of the street.

Tim Turn right here. Go along the road for about 200 metres. Left at the traffic lights. Go straight on for about 300 metres. Big building on the left. OK, I've got it. Thanks very much.

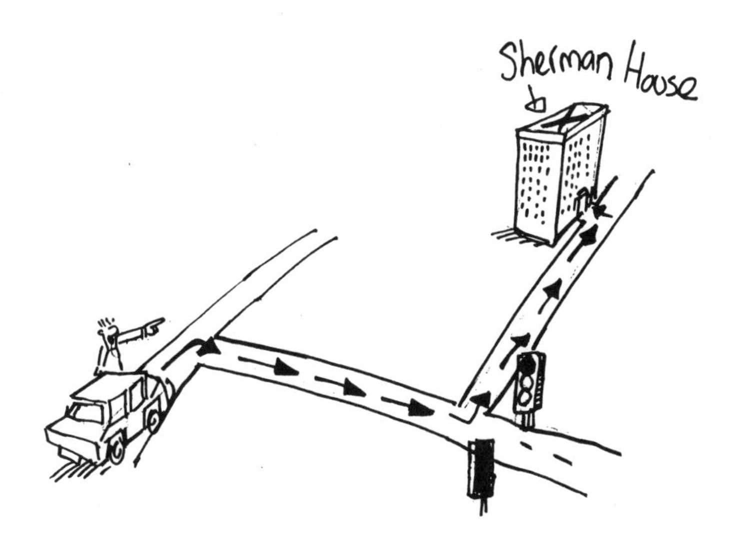

Which? The one . . .

Which animal is the fastest? The **one** on the left.
Which animal is the biggest? The **one** in the middle.
Which animals are the tallest? The **ones** on the right.

Charlie	Amy, would you like a sweet?
Amy	Yes, please. I'd love one.
Charlie	OK, which hand is it in?
Amy	The left one?
Charlie	Correct! Here you are.

Prof. English	You can say *The animal on the left* and *The animal on the right.* But we often say *The one on the left* or *The one on the right,* because it's shorter. You can say *I'd love one,* or *Which hand? The left one,* because you don't want to say *cake* or *hand* again. **One** is a very useful word.
Max	I've got three cakes here. Which one do you want?
Kit	The biggest one, please!

Which one?

Barbara wants a new shirt. She sees one in a shop window. She goes into the shop and speaks to the assistant.

Barbara	Excuse me. How much is that shirt in the window?
Assistant	Which one?
Barbara	The red one with little yellow and white flowers.
Assistant	It's £62.99, madam.
Barbara	Wow! That's expensive!

Assistant	There **are** cheaper ones. Look – do you like this one? It's very nice, it's red, and it's only £19.99.
	Brenda comes in.
Brenda	Hello, Barbara. What are **you** doing here?
Barbara	Buying a shirt, mum.
Brenda	*(very quietly)* This is a very expensive shop, Barbara. There's a cheaper one in Crown Street . . .
Barbara	*(loudly, to the assistant)* May I try the red one with little yellow and white flowers, please?

try

Exercises

A Look at the picture of cats and . . .
put a cross (×) beside the biggest one;
put a tick (√) beside the smallest one;
put a star (*) beside the prettiest one;
put an exclamation mark (!) beside the youngest one;
put a question mark (?) beside the oldest one;
put an O beside the black one;
put an F beside the fattest one.

B Now answer the questions.

Example: 1 Which cat is white?
The one on the right.

1 Which cat is white?
2 Which one is the youngest?
3 Which one is the most beautiful?
4 Which one is the fattest?
5 Which one is the biggest?
6 Which one is the smallest?
7 Which one is black?
8 Which one is the oldest?
9 Which one has the longest tail?

some biscuits

Prof. English I've got some biscuits. There are some biscuits on this plate.

Max How many?

Prof. English Oh, I don't know . . . *(He counts them.)* Sixteen.
Some means *a number of*. **Some** also means *a piece of*, *a kilo of*, etc.

Prof. English Some things are **countable**. You can count them: one, two, three cucumbers. We say ***There are*** *some cucumbers.* Coffee, sugar, water and money are **uncountable**. You can't count sugar and you can't count water.

Max You can count money!

Prof. English OK, OK, you can count coins and notes, but **money** is an uncountable noun. So we say ***There is*** *some money, some sugar or some water.*
Watch Max and Kit.

a cabbage some cabbage

Max Here's **a** cabbage. Now watch me. I'm cutting it into little pieces. I'm putting the pieces in a pan. Now I've got **some** cabbage. Let's cook it.

Kit We need **some** water, **some** butter and **some** salt.

Max How much water?

Kit Oh, about a quarter of a litre.

a cucumber some cucumber

a cake some cake

a chicken some chicken

How much? How many?

Prof. English	We say *How* **many** *cabbages have you got?* But we say *How* **much** *coffee have you got?*
Max	We don't say *How many money have you got?*
Kit	And we don't say *How much bananas have you got?*
Prof. English	That's right. We say *How many?* with countable things and *How much?* with uncountable things.

Exercises

C Look at the picture and write about it.
Example: *There are some apples. There is some wine.*

D Now look at the picture again and ask some questions, but do not write any answers!
Example: *How many apples are there? How much wine is there?*

17 Everyone has a birthday

any

Kit	Have you got any money, Professor?
Prof. English	Yes, I've got some money. I've got £21.65.
Kit	What about you, Max? Have you got any money?
Max	Yes, I've got some money too. I've got £3.21.
Kit	You're lucky! I haven't any money . . . Oh, yes, I have! I've got 15p.
Prof. English	In questions, we say **any**: *Have you got **any** money? Has Max got **any** sweets?* In "yes" sentences, when we have three or more of something countable, or some of something uncountable, we say **some**. *Yes, I've got **some** money. Yes, he has **some** sweets.*
Max	Or *Yes, I've got **some***, or *Yes, he's got **some***.
Kit	Why three or more?
Prof. English	Well, I've got one tree and two seats in my garden. Ask me about them.
Kit	OK. Have you got any trees in your garden?
Prof. English	Yes, I have. I've got one tree. Ask me about the seats.
Kit	OK, OK. Have you got any seats in your garden?
Prof. English	Yes, I've got two seats in my garden.
Kit	OK. Thank you.
Prof. English	That's right. And in "no" answers, we say **any**. *No, I haven't got **any** money. He hasn't got **any** sweets.*
Max	Or *No, I haven't got **any***, or *No, he hasn't got **any***.

sweets

no

Prof. English	We say *There isn't **any** food* or *There is **no** food.*
Max	Food?
Prof. English	Oh, apples, bread, eggs, chicken, soup – food . . . We say *I haven't **any** money* or *I have **no** money.* We don't usually write *There is not any food* or *I have not any money.*

Write  **Say**

Write	Say
There is no food.	There isn't any food. / There's no food.
There are no eggs.	There aren't any eggs. / There are no eggs.

Exercise

A Look at the picture on page 135 again and answer these questions.

Examples: 1 Is there any wine? *Yes, there is some wine.*
2 Is there any milk? *No, there is no milk.*

1 Is there any wine?
2 Is there any milk?
3 Are there any cherries?
4 Are there any cucumbers?
5 Is there any sugar?
6 Are there any apples?
7 Are there any eggs?
8 Is there any flour?
9 Is there any cabbage?
10 Are there any cabbages?
11 Is there any champagne?
12 Is there any cake?

empty and full

There is no milk in this bottle. It is **empty**. It is an empty bottle.
There is lots of milk in this bottle. It is **full**. It is a full bottle. It is full of milk.
This bus is empty. There are no people in it. It is an empty bus.
This bus is full. It is a full bus. It is full of people.

Prof. English You can say *This bus is full* or *This bus is full of people.* But you can't say *This bus is empty of people.* That's wrong.

There isn't any bread

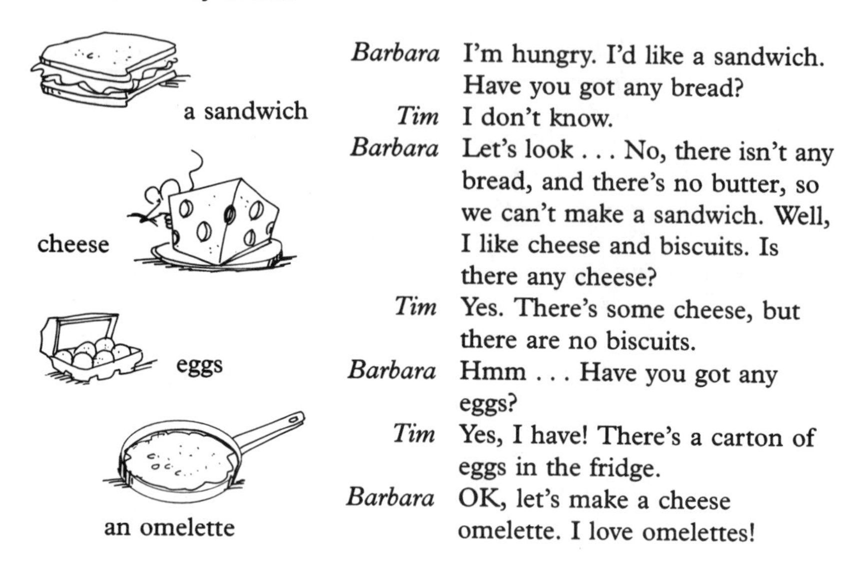

Barbara	I'm hungry. I'd like a sandwich. Have you got any bread?
Tim	I don't know.
Barbara	Let's look . . . No, there isn't any bread, and there's no butter, so we can't make a sandwich. Well, I like cheese and biscuits. Is there any cheese?
Tim	Yes. There's some cheese, but there are no biscuits.
Barbara	Hmm . . . Have you got any eggs?
Tim	Yes, I have! There's a carton of eggs in the fridge.
Barbara	OK, let's make a cheese omelette. I love omelettes!

because and so

We can't have dinner **because** we haven't any food.
We haven't any food, **so** we can't have dinner.
We can't make a sandwich **because** we haven't any bread.
We haven't any bread, **so** we can't make a sandwich.

a little, not much, a lot of

There is a little sugar in this jar.
There is not much sugar in this jar.

There is a lot of sugar in this jar.

a few, not many, a lot of

There are only a few biscuits on this plate.
There are not many biscuits on this plate.

There are a lot of biscuits on this plate.

Prof. English
You can say *There is not much sugar* or *There is a little sugar.* And you can say *There are not many biscuits* or *There are a few biscuits.*

a lot of, lots of

Kit	I like lots of sugar in my tea.
Max	I like a lot of sugar too.
Prof. English	*Lots of* and *a lot of* are the same. But we usually write *a lot of* and we say *lots of*. And we never say *a lots of*. That's not correct. **Only** is a useful word. We often say *only* when we're talking about a little or a few: *There's lots of sugar, but **only** a little tea. Lots of people can play football, but **only** a few people can play the double bass really well.*

Is there any flour?

Yes, there is
some flour
a little butter
a lot of bread
lots of bread

Are there any eggs?

Yes, there are
some eggs
a few cakes
a lot of people
lots of people

Exercise

B Look again at the picture on page 135 and write about it.
Example: *There are a lot of eggs but there is only one cucumber.*

more and most

Max has more cherries than Kit. The Professor has the most.

Kit has more cake than Max. The Professor has the most.

both of, all of

Max	**Both of** these oranges are bad. This one's bad, and that one's bad too. I can't eat them. Oh dear!
Prof. English	**All of** these apples are bad! I can't eat them.
Kit	Well, that's OK. I don't like apples. What about your cheese, Max? Is that OK? Can you eat **any** of that?
Max	No, it isn't. **All of** my cheese is bad. I can't eat it.
Kit	Never mind. Let's go out for a pizza!

some of

Prof. English — Two things or people: **both,** three or more things or people: **all.** You can say *both of* or *both.* You can say *all of* or *all.*

Max — OK, Professor – now look at these cherries. I've got five good ones and six bad ones. What do I say?

Prof. English — You say ***Some of*** *these cherries are bad.* You **never** say *Some these cherries are bad.* You need *of.* Now try it with this cabbage.

Max — ***Some of*** *this cabbage is bad, but* ***some of*** *it is OK.* I can cut the bad pieces out. I can cook the good pieces.

Prof. English — That's wonderful. Why aren't you a teacher?

Max — I'm too clever!

Some of these children are wearing T-shirts and **some of** them are wearing jumpers. The boys are **both** wearing shorts and the girls are **all** wearing skirts. The children are **all** wearing shoes.

Prof. English — You can say ***Both of*** *the boys are wearing shorts* or ***Both*** *the boys are wearing shorts.* You can also say *The boys are* ***both*** *wearing shorts.* You can say ***All*** *the children are wearing shoes* or ***All of*** *the children are wearing shoes.* You can also say *The children are* ***all*** *wearing shoes.* OK?

Abraham Lincoln

Kit — That's difficult.

Prof. English — Don't worry. Listen to President Lincoln's words:
"You can fool all the people some of the time. And you can fool some of the people all the time. But you can't fool all the people all the time."

fool

All Cows Eat Grass

Prof. English	In music, the notes have letters. Here are A, C, E and G. We say *All Cows Eat Grass.*
Max	Wrong! Not all cows eat grass; some cows eat turnips!
Prof. English	Do all engineers build bridges and tunnels? No, they don't. Not all engineers build bridges. Some engineers work with computers and telephones.

all and everybody/everyone

It is Amy's birthday. **All** the children **are** wearing paper hats. **Everybody is** wearing a paper hat. **Everyone is** singing "Happy Birthday".
Does Amy have a birthday party every month?
No, but she has one every year. Nearly everybody has a birthday every year.
Nearly everybody? Yes. Joe has a birthday party every four years. Why?

His birthday is on 29 February.

Kit I love ice cream. Everybody likes ice cream.

Max You're wrong. Not everyone likes ice cream. Lots of people hate it.

Prof. English You can say **everybody** or **everyone**. Both are OK.

Charlie Dad, please may I have some new Superfast trainers?

Harry I don't know. How much do they cost?

Charlie Sixty pounds.

Harry Sixty pounds! You can buy trainers for twenty pounds.

Charlie Yes, dad, but Superfast trainers are special. Everybody's wearing them.

Harry Everybody? There are twenty boys and girls in your class. Has every child in your class got a pair of Superfast trainers?

Charlie Well, Tony Moore's got a pair.

Harry Tony Moore's father's rich. Sorry, Charlie, the answer is no.

everything

Max is going on holiday. He is putting everything into his bag.

Prof. English **Everything** is like **all the things**. Everything in this book is useful.

Max But not everything is interesting!

somebody

The door bell is ringing.

Harry	There's somebody at the door. Can you answer it, Brenda? I'm busy.
Salesman	Good evening. Would you like to buy a new washing machine?
Brenda	Well . . .
Harry	Who is it, Brenda?
Brenda	Somebody wants to sell us a washing machine.

Prof. English We say **somebody**, or **someone**, when we don't know who the person is. Both **somebody** and **someone** are OK.

something

Amy	I've got something in my eye.
Brenda	Well, open your eye . . . Yes, there's something there.
Amy	What is it?
Brenda	It's only an eyelash . . . There, I've got it. Does your eye feel all right now?
Amy	Yes, thank you. It feels fine.

anything and nothing

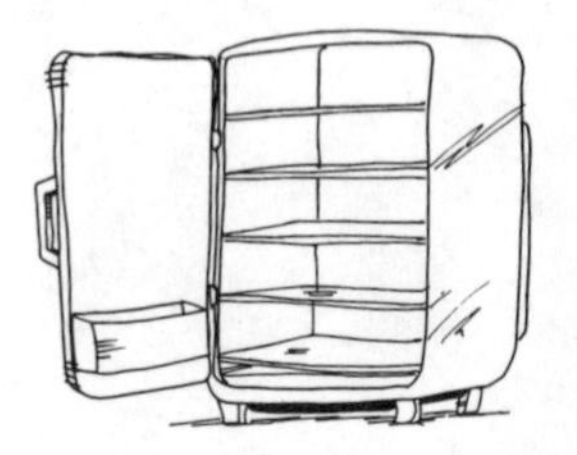

Barbara	Is there anything in the fridge?
Tim	No, there isn't.
Barbara	Is there really nothing in the fridge?
Tim	That's right. There's no food. The fridge is empty.
Barbara	OK. Let's go out for a pizza.

Prof. English
Here, **anything** means *any food.* In questions, we say *Is there **anything** in the fridge?* In "yes" sentences we say *There is **something** in the fridge.* In "no" sentences we say ***There isn't anything** in the fridge* or ***There's nothing** in the fridge.*

Exercises

C There is not much food in this fridge.
Look at the shelves and answer the questions.

Example: 1 Is there anything on the top shelf? *Yes, there is. There are some eggs on the top shelf.*

1 Is there anything on the top shelf?
2 Is there anything on the second shelf?
3 Is there anything on the middle shelf?
4 Is there anything on the fourth shelf?
5 Is there anything on the bottom shelf?

D Right or wrong? Put a tick (√) beside the correct sentences. Put a cross (×) beside the wrong ones and write the correct answers beside them.

Examples:
1 Everybody has a nose. (√)
2 Everybody has brown eyes.
(×) *Not everybody has brown eyes.*
Can you write something interesting?
Example:
Some people have black, blue, green or grey eyes.

1 Everybody has a nose.
2 Everybody has brown eyes.
3 Nobody likes snakes.
4 Everyone has a name.
5 Everyone likes pizza.
6 All cows eat grass.
7 All cars have four wheels.

18 I feel fine!

anybody, anyone; nobody, no one

Kit	Is there anybody there?
	There is no answer.
Max	What's the matter?
Kit	There isn't anybody there.
Max	Hello, is there anyone there?
	There is no answer.
Max	There's no one there.

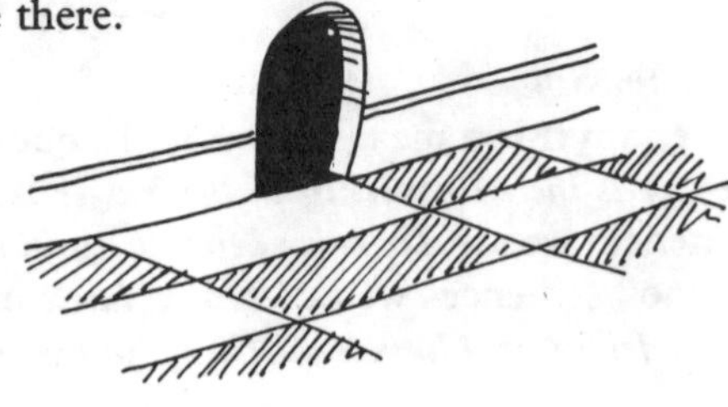

Prof. English
It's always **any** in questions: *Is there* ***anybody*** *here? Is there* ***anyone*** *at home?*
In "yes" sentences it's always **somebody** or **someone**. *There's* ***somebody*** *outside. There's* ***someone*** *at the door.*
In "no" sentences we say *There isn't* ***anybody/anyone*** *there*, or *There's* ***nobody/no one*** *there.*
Anybody, anyone and **nobody** are all one word. **No one** is two words.

Exercise

A Write *somebody/someone, nobody/no one* or *anybody/anyone* in the spaces.

Example: 1 Is there *anybody/anyone* at home? No, there's *nobody/no one* at home.

1 Is there .... at home? No, there's .... at home.
2 .... is drinking my milk!
3 Has .... got my bag?
4 .... loves me because I'm ugly!
5 .... loves me – they send me flowers every week!
6 There isn't .... in the shop. It's empty.

The body

Prof. English In *Is anybody there?*, **body** means *person*. But everybody has **a body**.

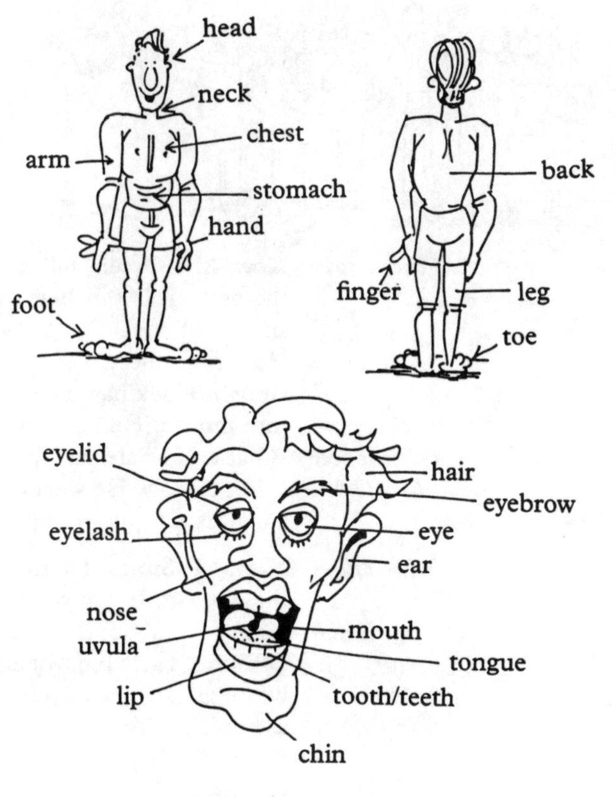

Prof. English This is *a hair*, and this is *hair*. My hair is brown. Some people have black hair. Some have yellow hair – we say *blond hair*. A lot of Swedes and Norwegians have blond hair. Some old people have grey or white hair. Some people have red hair.

Max Red like a tomato?

Prof. English No, no. Red like autumn leaves.

Baby A's hair is short and straight. Baby B's hair is long and curly.

Exercises

B Who are they talking about?

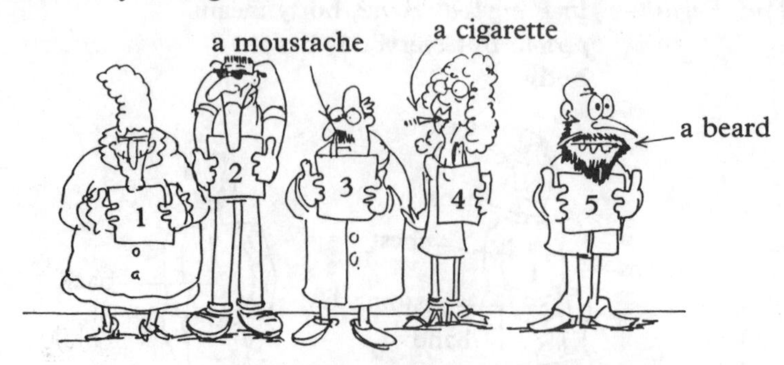

Police officer	Now, Mrs Green, tell me about the person. Is this person tall or short?
Mrs Green	He's tall, officer. He has short, straight black hair and a long, thin mouth. He has a big nose.
Police officer	What colour are his eyes?
Mrs Green	I don't know. He wears sunglasses.
Police officer	Now, Mr Smith, tell me about the woman. Is she young or old?
Mr Smith	Young . . . about 25 or 30. She has long, curly blond hair. She wears glasses. Her eyebrows are very blond. You can't really see them. She has big red lips and she always has a cigarette in her mouth.
Police officer	Now, Mr French, tell me about the person. Is it a man or a woman?
Mr French	I don't know, but the person has a big black beard!
Police officer	OK, OK, that's very funny. Does he wear glasses?
Mr French	No. He's got very big, black eyes. His nose is long and thin. His mouth is long and thin too. He has very bad, ugly teeth.

C There are five pictures here. Write about the other two!

with

He is a tall man. He has a long nose.
He is a tall man **with** a long nose.

There is a man here. He is carrying a piano.
There is a man **with** a piano here.

Harry	Please can you help me? I'm looking for my son.
Policeman	How old is he, and what does he look like?
Harry	He's four. He's shorter than I am, with blond hair and blue eyes.
Policeman	What's he wearing?
Harry	Blue trousers, a white shirt and green and white trainers.

A very silly joke

Kit	There's a man at the door with a black beard.
Max	Say "No, thank you. We don't want to buy any beards today!"

It hurts!

Charlie's leg hurts.

Exercises

D Write the words on the pictures.

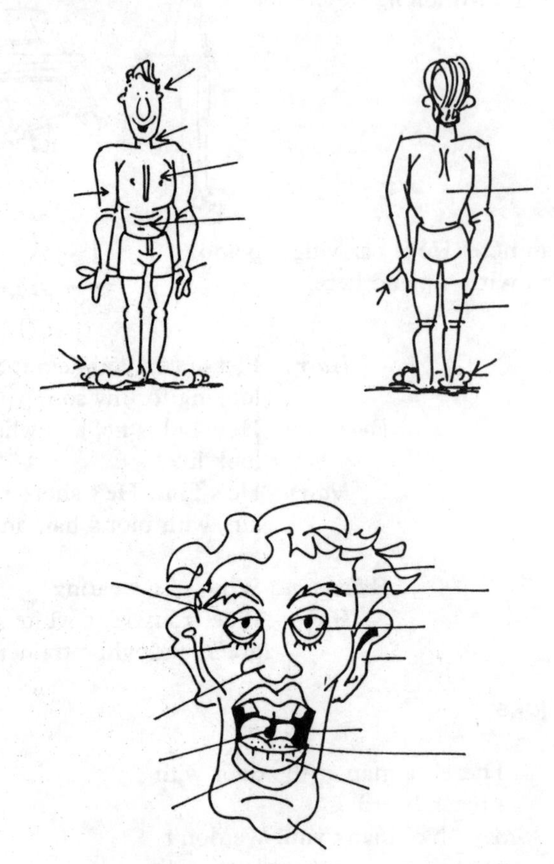

E Write sentences.
Example: leg – *My leg hurts!*

leg, eyes, back, nose, head, feet, teeth,
left ear, right arm, chest, stomach,
hand, toes, finger, ears, neck

I feel ill

Prof. English Usually I feel well, but sometimes I feel ill. I'm feeling OK today. We can say *I'm feeling well* or *I feel well.* Both are OK.

Prof. English **All right** is like *OK*. I'm feeling all right today.
Kit Let's play tennis, Professor!
Prof. English All right, Kit.

ache

Prof. English Look at the queue of people. We can say *My head **aches*** or *My head **is aching***. Both are OK. We often say *I've got **a** headache, I've got **a** stomach ache*, but we usually say *I've got toothache* and *I've got earache* – no **a**.
Max Why?
Prof. English I don't know.

Harry is ill

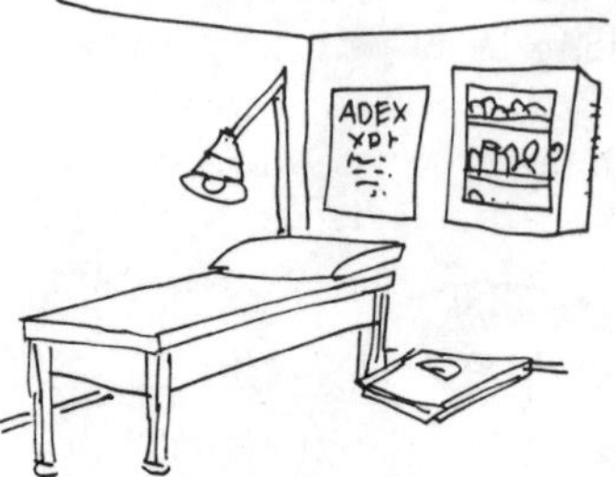

a surgery

Brenda Get up, Harry! It's nearly half past eight.

Harry I can't get up. I'm too ill. I feel sick, my chest hurts, my eyes ache, my head aches and I feel terrible.

Brenda Oh dear. Poor Harry!

She telephones the doctor.

Harry What are you doing?

Brenda I'm telephoning the surgery. It opens at half past eight.

Receptionist Hello. Surgery. Can I help you?

Brenda Yes, please. My husband isn't feeling well. He feels sick, his chest hurts, his eyes ache and he's got a headache.

a receptionist

Receptionist Whose patient is he?

Brenda Doctor Potter's.

Receptionist Doctor Potter's very busy. Can your husband come to the surgery, please?

Harry I can't go to the surgery! I'm too ill.

Brenda You're well enough to sit in the car. *(to the receptionist)* I can drive him to the surgery.

Receptionist Good. Please come at half past ten. What's your husband's name, please?

Brenda Harry Williams . . . Come on, Harry. Put your clothes on, please. We're going to the surgery.

a doctor a patient

Receptionist Name, please.

Harry Harry Williams.

Receptionist Take this ticket and sit down in the waiting-room, please.

a waiting-room

Harry There's a long queue. I'm number 22.

Brenda No, there isn't. Look, number 17's with the doctor now. There are only five people in front of you. Would you like to read a magazine?

Harry No, thank you. I don't feel well enough.

Doctor Potter Good morning, Mr Williams. I'm Della Potter. Can I help you?

a magazine

Harry I feel terrible, doctor. I feel sick and I've got a headache, my chest hurts and my eyes ache.

Doctor Potter Take off your shirt, please . . . Well, Mr Williams, you've got flu. Here's a prescription. Please take it to the chemist and get your medicine. Take one teaspoonful every four hours.

a prescription

Harry Can I go to work?

Doctor Potter Do you feel well enough to go to work?

Harry No, I don't. I want to go to bed!

Doctor Potter OK. Go to bed and have lots of hot drinks. Goodbye, and get well soon.

medicine

An ill person is called a **patient**. In Britain, doctors sometimes come to their patients' homes, but patients often go to the surgery. The doctor gives them a prescription for medicine. They take the prescription to the chemist and get their medicine. Most people pay for their medicine, but children and very poor people do not pay.

Exercise

F Here is Doctor Potter's list of patients. Write about them.

Example: 1 *Ms Down is 21 years old. She has a headache. Her eyes hurt and she often feels tired.*

1 Ms Down: age 21, head aches, eyes hurt, often feels tired.
2 Peter East: age 11, ears hurt.
3 Mr Potter: age 78, back, neck and arms hurt.
4 Miss Brown: age 52, stomach hurts, chest hurts.

19 Who were they?

today and yesterday

Today is the 28th of May and the weather is sunny.
Yesterday was the 27th of May. The weather was very wet.

Prof. English *The weather* ***is*** *sunny* is the **present tense**. *The weather* ***was*** *wet* is the **past tense**.

Yesterday Max **was** ill. Now he is well again.
In 1944 I **was** a baby. Now I'm a man.
On 12 January Kit and Max **were** in London.
Now they are at home.

Write and say

I/he/she/it **was**	**was** I/he/she/it?
you/we/they **were**	**were** you/we/they?
Write	**Say**
I/he/she/it **was not**	I/he/she/it **wasn't**
you/we/they **were not**	you/we/they **weren't**

Harry Look at these old photographs.
Brenda Look – here's a photo of Amy!
Harry Oh, yes. She was three years old.
Brenda No, she wasn't. She was two. There's a date on the back of the photo. And now Amy's ten years old!
Harry Oh, yes. We were on holiday in France.
Brenda No, Harry. We weren't in France. We were in Spain.
Harry Oh, yes. The hotel was very good.
Brenda No, Harry. The hotel wasn't very good. But the weather was hot and sunny every day and the children were very happy.

Exercise

A Look at this time line and answer the questions.
Example: 1 *In 1944 he was one year old.*

1 How old was the Professor in 1944?
2 How old was he in 1960?
3 And how old is he now?
4 Where was he in 1953?
5 When was he in hospital?
6 Where was he in May 1961?
7 Where was he in 1964?
8 Where was he in 1973?
9 How old was he in 1978?

at school in Africa at Cambridge University
in France in London in hospital

ago

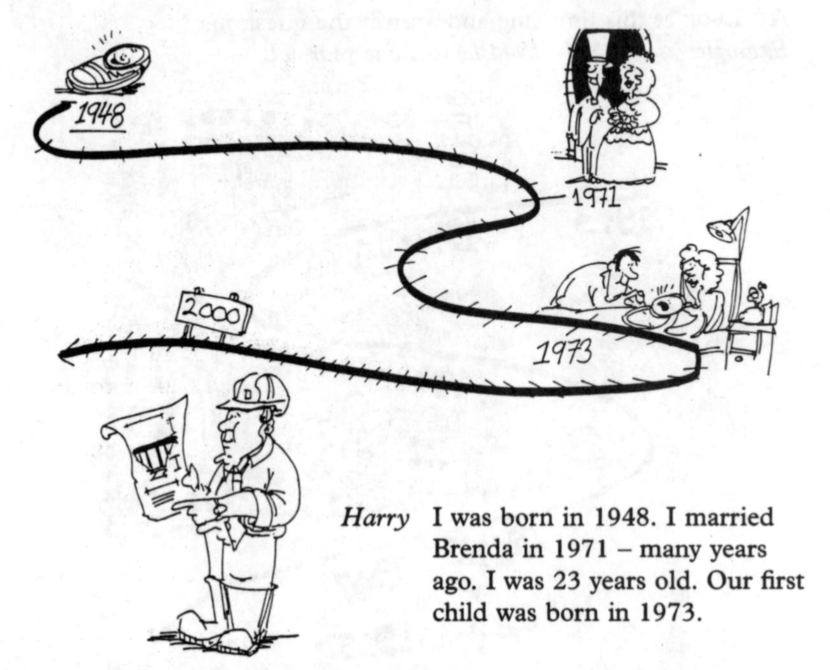

Harry I was born in 1948. I married Brenda in 1971 – many years ago. I was 23 years old. Our first child was born in 1973.

Prof. English Now you! Where were you twenty years ago? Ten years ago? Five years ago?

last night, last Thursday

had

Prof. English	Kit, you usually have milk for breakfast, and you had milk for breakfast this morning.
Kit	That's right. How do you know?
Prof. English	There's some milk on your face!

a sausage

Reporter	Excuse me, did you have breakfast this morning?
Man	Yes, I did. I had two slices of toast and a cup of tea.
Woman	I had sausages and tomatoes and lots of black coffee.
Boy	I had eggs and toast and a glass of milk.
Girl	No, I didn't have any breakfast this morning. I never eat breakfast. I'm always too busy.

I/You/He/She/It/We/They **had** breakfast.
I/You/He/She/It/We/They **did not have** breakfast.
Did I/you/he/she/it/we/they **have** breakfast?
Yes, I/you/he/she/it/we/they **did**.
No, I/you/he/she/it/we/they **did not/didn't**.

Where **did** you **have** breakfast? In the kitchen.
What **did** you **have** for breakfast? Tea and toast.
When **did** you **have** it? At eight o'clock.

Exercise

B Read the questions again. Now write these conversations.

Example:	*Reporter:*	*Did you have breakfast this morning?*
	Joe:	*Yes, I did.*
	Reporter:	*What did you have for breakfast?*
	Joe:	*I had . . .*
	Reporter:	*When . . .?*

Joe: Yes. 7 a.m. In the kitchen. Coffee, toast and jam.
Sally: No. Late for work.
Colin: Yes. In bed (ill). 9 a.m. Tea and toast.
Peter: Yes. In the dining room. Sausages, eggs, tomatoes, toast, orange juice, coffee.

orange juice

Who was I?

Prof. English — Let's play a game. Listen! I was a famous author. I was born in England in 1564. I married Anne Hathaway in 1582. My most famous plays are *Romeo and Juliet*, *Hamlet*, *Macbeth* and *King Lear*. I died in England in 1616. Who was I?

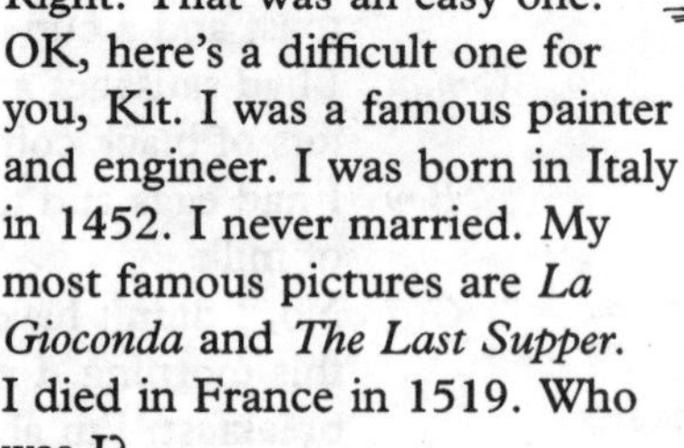

Max — William Shakespeare?

Prof. English — Right. That was an easy one. OK, here's a difficult one for you, Kit. I was a famous painter and engineer. I was born in Italy in 1452. I never married. My most famous pictures are *La Gioconda* and *The Last Supper*. I died in France in 1519. Who was I?

Kit — Hmm. You were a painter **and** an engineer?

Prof. English — That's right.

Kit — I don't know. Max, do you know the answer?

Max — Leonardo da Vinci. That was an easy one. Ask us another one, Professor.

Kit — This game's too boring. Let's play football!

Exercise

C Now you do it! Write "Who was I?" for three famous people. What about Queen Victoria, Marilyn Monroe, Abraham Lincoln, Pablo Picasso, Marie Curie, Charlie Chaplin?
Some of these people had long lives. Some of them had short lives. All of them had interesting lives. Can you write about them? When were they born? Who did they marry? When did they die?

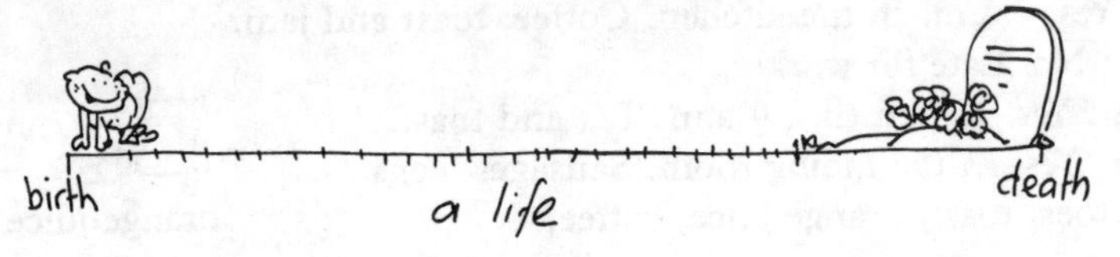

lived and worked

Prof. English
William Shakespeare was born in Stratford upon Avon. He **lived** and **worked** in London. *Live* and *work* are **regular** verbs.
We add **ed** to regular verbs like *work:*
Shakespeare ***worked*** *in London.*
We add **d** to regular verbs like *live* and *die:*
Shakespeare ***lived*** *in England; Leonardo* ***died*** *in France.*
We take off the **y** off regular verbs like *marry* and add **ied**: *William Shakespeare* ***married*** *Anne Hathaway; the baby* ***cried*** *last night.*

> I/you/he/she/it/we/they **lived**
> **did** I/you/he/she/it/we/they **live**?
> I/you/he/she/it/we/they **did not/didn't live**

Questions

When **was** William Shakespeare **born**? He **was born** in 1564.
Was he born in London? No, he was not.
He **was born** in Stratford upon Avon.
What **did** Shakespeare **do** for a living? **Was he** a painter?
No. He **was** a writer.
Where **did** he **work**? He **worked** in London.
Who **did** he **marry**? He **married** Anne Hathaway.
When **did** Shakespeare **die**? He **died** in 1616.
Did he die in London? No, he did not.
He died in Stratford upon Avon.

Lady Bracknell I always say ***Whom*** *did he marry?*

Prof. English That's correct, but it sounds very old-fashioned. I always **write** *Whom did he marry?*, but it's OK to **say** *Who did he marry?*

start . . . ing, stop . . . ing

Prof. English	I started smoking in 1964. I stopped smoking in 1965. I smoked from 1964 to 1965. I don't smoke now.
Kit	What did you smoke?
Prof. English	Cigarettes.
Max	Did you smoke every day?
Prof. English	Yes. I smoked ten cigarettes a day.

from . . . to; for

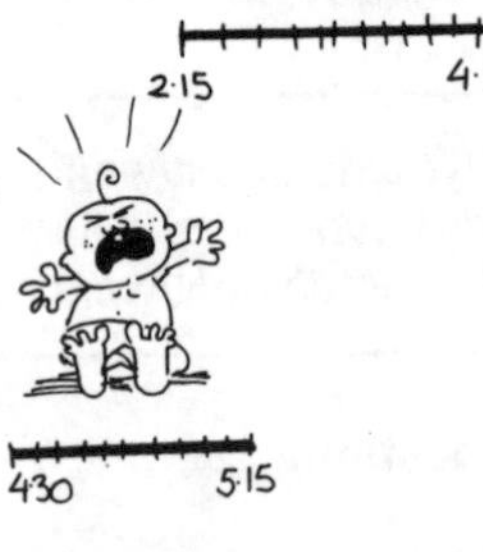

Mr Duncan started playing his double bass at 2.15. He stopped playing at 4.15. He played his double bass **from** 2.15 **to** 4.15. He played his double bass **for** 2 hours.
The baby started crying at 4.30. She stopped crying at 5.15. She cried **from** 4.30 **to** 5.15. She cried **for** 45 minutes.
The shop opened at 9 a.m. It closed at 5.30 p.m. It was open **from** 9 a.m. **to** 5.30 p.m. It was open **for** 8½ hours.

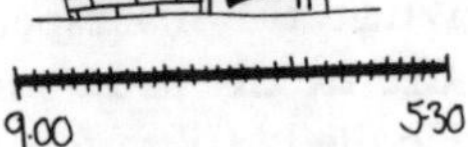

Prof. English	You can also say **until**: *I worked from 9 o'clock **until** 6 o'clock. The shop is open **until** 5.30.*

Exercise

D Read these notes and write sentences. Use *from, to/until* (both are OK) and *for*.
Example: 1 *Professor English talked from two o'clock to/until three o'clock. He talked for an hour.*

1 Professor English – talk – 2 p.m. – 3 p.m.
2 The baby – cry – 1.30 p.m. – 4 p.m.
3 Charlie – play CDs – 9 p.m. – 11.30 p.m.
4 James – watch TV – 6.15 p.m. – 7.25 p.m.
5 Harry – work in California – 1 June – 1 September.
6 Kit – be ill – Monday morning – Wednesday night.
7 Brenda – live in London – 1973 – 1978.
8 Tim – clean car – 3.15 – 4.20.
9 Amy – play in tree house – 10 a.m. – 3 p.m.
10 Mr Duncan – play double bass – 7 30 p.m. – 11 p.m.

a long time, a short time

Barbara worked **for a long time** yesterday.
James and Charlie played chess **for a short time** yesterday.
1875 was **a long time** ago.

a moment

Prof. English **A moment** is usually a very short time – like a second. But when Barbara says "Wait a moment", *a moment* can mean *half an hour*!

then

Tim What did you do today, Barbara?
Barbara I worked from 8 a.m. to 6 p.m., then I cleaned my taxi.
Tim What did you do then? Did you watch TV?
Barbara No. I visited Jane. She was in Spain until last week, but now she's at home again. We looked at her holiday photos for half an hour, then she cooked a Spanish omelette.

How long . . . ?

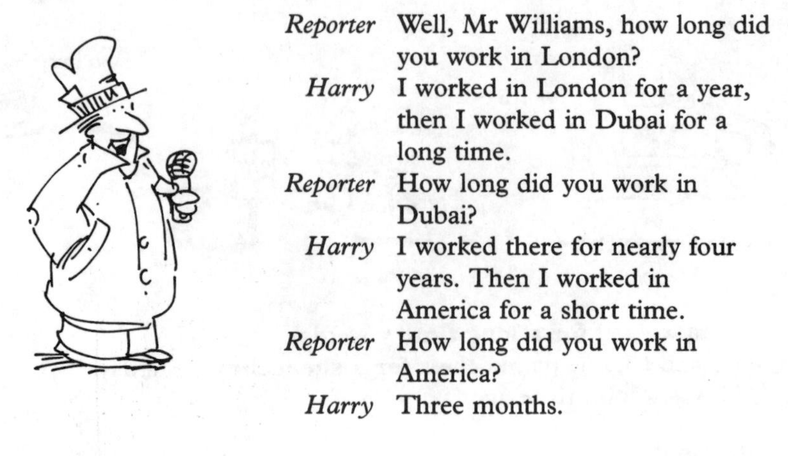

Reporter Well, Mr Williams, how long did you work in London?

Harry I worked in London for a year, then I worked in Dubai for a long time.

Reporter How long did you work in Dubai?

Harry I worked there for nearly four years. Then I worked in America for a short time.

Reporter How long did you work in America?

Harry Three months.

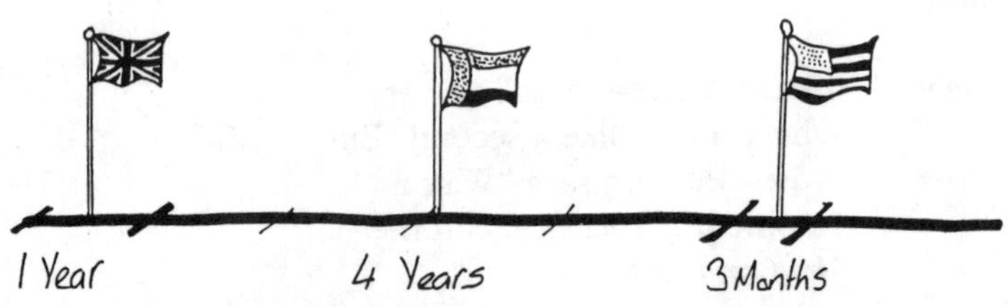

Exercises

E Here are some lives of famous people, with their dates. Write their lives.

1 Mahatma Gandhi: Statesman. Born in India in 1869. Lived in London and South Africa. Came back to India in 1918. Died in India in 1948.
2 Marco Polo: Traveller. Born in Italy in 1254. Travelled to China with his father in 1271. Lived in China for many years. Died in Italy in 1324.
3 Wolfgang Amadeus Mozart: Composer. Born in Austria in 1756. Composed his first piece of music at the age of 5. Travelled with his father and sister to Germany, France, England and Italy. Married in 1782. Six children. Four died. Composed hundreds of pieces of music but was always poor. Died in 1791.

F Write about these shops.

Example: 1 *The book shop is open from 9 a.m. to 5.30 p.m. It closes for lunch at 12.30 p.m. for an hour. It opens again at 1.30 p.m. and it closes again at 5.30 p.m.*

1 Book shop: 9–12.30, 1.30–5.30
2 Dress shop: 9.30–12.30, 2–5.30
3 Shoe shop: 9–1, 2.30–5
4 Newsagent: 7.30–5.30

Newsagents sell newspapers, magazines, sweets and cigarettes.

G Put the correct words in the spaces.

Example: Mr Duncan *wanted* to go to the station.

Mr Duncan's day

Mr Duncan .... to go to the station. (want)
He .... to catch the 6.30 train to London. (need)
He .... Barbara. (phone)
"Can you take me to the station?" he .... (ask)
"Of course," .... Barbara. (answer)
She .... at Mr Duncan's house at 5.30 a.m. in her taxi. (arrive)
She .... the taxi door and .... him with his double bass. (open, help)
They .... at the station and Barbara .... her taxi in the car park. (arrive, park)
She .... goodbye to Mr Duncan. (wave)
Mr Duncan .... in London. (arrive)
He .... in a concert, then he .... dinner with the other musicians. (play, have)
He .... very tired. (be)

20 Once upon a time

Cathy's day

Reporter Hello, and welcome to *Busy People*. This is Cathy. Cathy, what do you do for a living?

Cathy I was a receptionist, but I married Jim four years ago and now I'm a wife and mother.

Reporter What did you do yesterday, Cathy?

Cathy I shopped. I cooked. I played with the children. I washed a lot of clothes. I mended some clothes. I cleaned the windows. I polished the furniture. I bathed the children . . . and now I'm very tired!

Prof. English
There are lots of regular verbs; but there are a lot of irregular ones too. Yesterday I **sat** down and **thought** about them. I **wrote** some sentences. Here they are!

Prof. English A few irregular verbs are the same in the past and in the present:

read – read: Amy **read** three books last week.
beat – beat: The cook **beat** the eggs and cooked them with a little butter and salt.
put – put: Brenda **put** the dirty clothes into the washing machine two hours ago.
cut – cut: Barbara **cut** the bread this morning.
hurt – hurt: Charlie **hurt** his leg last week and now he can't walk very well.
hit – hit: Last night Amy **hit** James with a cushion.
cost – cost: Barbara's new shoes were expensive. They **cost** £45.

Max But *I read a book yesterday* doesn't sound the same as *I read a book every day.*

Prof. English That's right. It looks the same, but it sounds different. In *I read a book every day*, **read** sounds like **need**. In *I read a very interesting book yesterday,* **read** sounds like **red** or **bed** . . .

Kit Or **head**!

the same

different

Prof. English There are some "families" of irregular verbs:

sit – sat: I **sat** on a sofa.
begin – began: The baby **began** to cry.
drink – drank: I **drank** three cups of tea.
swim – swam: Charlie **swam** half a kilometre last week.
ring – rang: The bell **rang**.
run – ran: The mouse **ran** into its hole.
sing – sang: Tim **sang** very noisily.

speak – spoke: I telephoned the hotel and **spoke** to the manager.
break – broke: Brenda **broke** a glass.

Max But **break** doesn't sound the same as **speak**.

Prof. English That's right. **Break** sounds like **take**, and **speak** sounds like **week**. They sound different, but they both look the same.

Prof. English Some verbs are different. Here are some of those verbs:

bite – bit: The dog **bit** Fred this morning.
blow – blew: The wind **blew** my hat off.
build – built: The engineers **built** a new bridge across the river.
buy – bought: Tim **bought** some new shoes last week.
catch – caught: The cat **caught** a rabbit.
come – came: Barbara **came** home very late last night.
dig – dug: The men **dug** a hole in the road.
draw – drew: Amy **drew** a picture of a cow.
drive – drove: Harry **drove** to Scotland last week.
eat – ate: I **ate** five biscuits.
fall – fell: Charlie **fell** off his bicycle.
feel – felt: I usually feel very well, but this morning I **felt** terrible.
fly – flew: The aeroplane **flew** to Dublin yesterday.
get – got: I **got** up at 6 a.m. this morning.
give – gave: Tim **gave** Barbara some flowers.
go – went: Last night Barbara **went** to a concert.
hear – heard: I **heard** a noise.
leave – left: Mr Duncan **left** home at eight o'clock.
make – made: Amy **made** eleven mistakes today.

pay – paid: Tim **paid** £15 for a bunch of flowers for Barbara.
say – said: "Hello," **said** Barbara.
see – saw: Amy **saw** a rainbow yesterday.

sleep – slept: Tim **slept** for a long time.
smell – smelt: The dirty old dog **smelt** terrible.
spend – spent: Brenda went to the shops and **spent** £120.
stand – stood: I **stood** and waited for a bus.
take – took: Brenda **took** the clean clothes out of the washing machine.
teach – taught: My mother **taught** me to swim.
tell – told: My mother **told** me a wonderful story about a boy and his cat.
write – wrote: I **wrote** a letter to my girlfriend.
wear – wore: Barbara **wore** her new shoes yesterday.

Exercise

A Put the right words in the spaces.
Example: 1 The dog *caught* a rabbit, then it *ate* it.

1 The dog .... (catch) a rabbit, then it .... (eat) it.
2 Brenda .... (write) a letter and .... (send) it to her mother.
3 Tim .... (make) a cup of tea and .... (drink) it.
4 Amy .... (buy) a pair of red sunglasses and .... (wear) them at school.
5 The bird .... (bite) me, then it .... (fly) away.
6 Harry .... (build) a bridge in Singapore, then he .... (leave) Singapore and .... (go) to Dubai.
7 James .... (fall) off his bicycle and .... (break) his nose.
8 Barbara .... (drive) to Mr Duncan's house and .... (take) him to a concert.
9 Charlie .... (feel) ill, so he .... (go) to the doctor.
10 Charlie .... (teach) Amy to play football and .... (buy) her a pair of football boots.

Prof. English There was a young lady called Jane
Who was terribly sick in a train,
Not once, but again
And again and again
And again and again and again!

Max I like that song. Please sing it again!

Kit No, don't sing it again. I travelled by train last week and I felt very sick.

Prof. English **Once** can mean *one time: I sang my song once*. But we use **once** in stories too. Lots of children's stories start "Once upon a time".

Max Tell us a story, Professor!

Kit Yes, please tell a story. I'd like a story about a cat.

Prof. English OK, this is the story of *Puss in Boots.*

Kit Puss?

Prof. English A long time ago, everybody called their cats Puss.

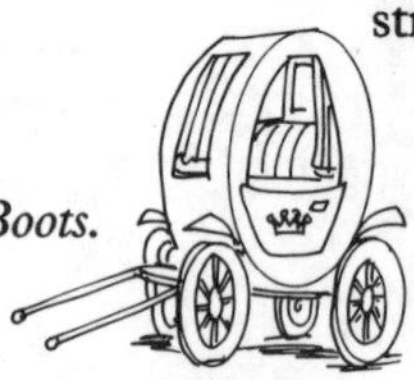

Max What did they call their mice?

Prof. English Mice didn't have names . . . Please listen to the story.

a servant

strong

a coach

drown

Once upon a time an old man lived in a little house in the country with his three sons. They were very poor. They only had one cow, one horse and a small black cat. One day the old man said to his sons, "I am dying." He gave the house to his first son, he gave the horse and the cow to his second son and he gave the cat to his youngest son. Then he closed his eyes and died.

"Let's work together," said the oldest son to the second son. They said to their brother, "We don't need you! You aren't old enough, and you aren't strong enough. Go away – and take your cat with you!"

The young man's name was Peter. He said to the cat, "Come on, Puss! Let's go to London. Perhaps I can get a job there."

"OK," said the cat. "But it's a long way to London. Please may I have some boots?"

"Puss, you can talk!" said Peter.

"Of course," said the cat. "I'm a very special cat. Now let's buy those boots," and they walked down the road together.

Well, cats do not usually wear boots, and Peter did not have much money, but they went together to a shoe shop and Peter bought a pair of beautiful red boots for his cat. Puss put his new boots on. He looked wonderful.

They walked and walked. One evening, they saw a sign.

"I can't read," said Puss. "What does the sign say?"

"It says LONDON 5 KILOMETRES," said Peter. "We're very near London now."

In the morning Puss got up very early and caught two fat young rabbits. He took them to the King's palace and knocked on the door. A servant opened the door.

"Good morning," said Puss. "I am Prince Peter's servant. He sent these rabbits for the King."

"Thank you," said the servant. He took the rabbits and closed the door.

The servant took the rabbits to the King. "A present from Prince Peter," he said.

"That's wonderful," said the King. "Take them to the kitchen, please . . . Who is Prince Peter?"

"I don't know," said the servant.

The next morning Puss got up early again. He caught two fat little birds and took them to the palace. Again he knocked at the door, and again he gave them to the servant. And again the King was very pleased. But who was Prince Peter? The King wanted to know.

The next day, Peter and Puss came to a river. Peter took off his old, dirty clothes and jumped into the cold, clean water. He swam happily for a long time and he washed his hair and cleaned his fingernails.

Then the King's beautiful coach came down the road. Puss saw it. Carefully he put Peter's old, dirty clothes in some long grass.

"Stay in the water for a moment," said Puss. Then he ran to the coach and shouted to the driver.

"Can anybody help me, please? The Prince is drowning!"

Peter heard him. He said, "Puss, don't be silly! I'm not drowning, and I'm not a prince!"

"Be quiet," said Puss.

The driver helped Peter out of the water. "Don't look," said Puss. "The Prince hasn't any clothes."

The King gave Peter some beautiful, expensive clothes. "You are cold and tired," he said. "Climb into my coach and come home with me." He looked at Puss. "You can come too, little cat," he said.

Prof. English	. . . Well, it's a long story, but Peter married the King's daughter.
Kit	What happened to the cat?
Prof. English	Peter gave him a new pair of boots every week, and he slept on Peter's bed every night.

a long way

Max	It's a long way to Tipperary, It's a long way to go, It's a long way to Tipperary, To the sweetest girl I know. Goodbye, Piccadilly, Farewell, Leicester Square, It's a long, long way to Tipperary, And my heart is there.
Kit	Where's Tipperary?
Max	I don't know. Where's Tipperary, Professor?
Prof. English	Tipperary is a town in Ireland. Soldiers sang that song in 1914 when they were in France. *Farewell* is an old-fashioned word for *Goodbye*. And Piccadilly and Leicester Square are streets in London.

a heart

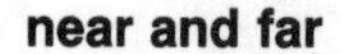

near and far

Prof. English
Look at this map. Eyke is **near** Woodbridge, but it is **a long way from** London. **How far** is it **from** Eyke **to** Woodbridge? About 6 kilometres. Eyke is about 150 kilometres **from** London.
Woodbridge is **not far from** Ipswich. **How far** is Woodbridge **from** Ipswich? About 8 kilometres.
Woodbridge is only about 8 kilometres **from** Ipswich.

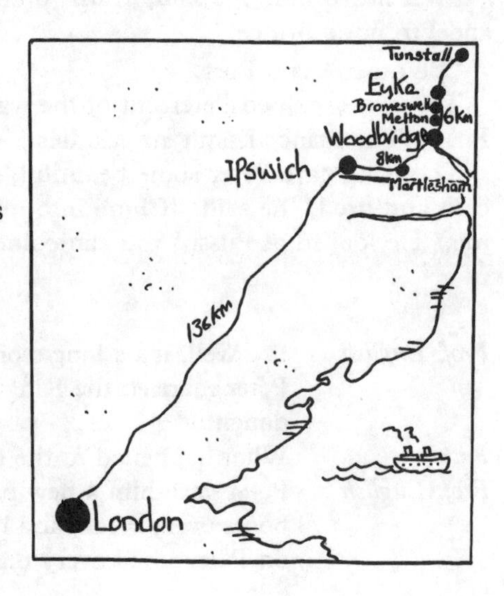

Exercises

B Look at the map again and write in the spaces.
Use *far, near, a long way.*

Example: 1 Eyke is *near* Woodbridge and it is not very *far* from Ipswich.

1 Eyke is .... Woodbridge and it is not very .... from Ipswich.
2 Tunstall is .... Bromeswell, but it is .... from London.
3 Martlesham is very .... Ipswich and not .... from Woodbridge.
4 Tunstall, Melton and Bromeswell are all very .... Eyke, but they are .... from London.

C Look again at pages 165 to 167, then write the verbs in the spaces. Be careful, nearly all of them are irregular!

Example: 1 She *sat* in the garden and *smelt* the flowers.

1 She .... (sit) in the garden and .... (smell) the flowers.
2 The firemen .... (ring) the bell, then .... (drive) their fire engine to the fire.
3 James .... (eat) two pizzas and .... (drink) a bottle of lemonade, then he .... (feel) sick.
4 Charlie .... (fall) off his bicycle and .... (hurt) his arm.
5 I .... (break) a plate, so I .... (buy) a new one.
6 The bird .... (take) a piece of bread and .... (fly) away.
7 Barbara .... (write) a long letter to Tim and .... (send) it in a big white envelope.
8 The cat .... (chase) a rabbit and .... (catch) it. Then he .... (take) it to the King.

lemonade

a country and the country

This is a country.

SPAIN

Prof. English	Spain is **a country**. But **the country** is different. **The country** is the opposite of **the town**.
Rosy	I live in the country. The nearest big town is Ipswich and I go there once or twice a month.

a house in the town

a house in the country

21 What are you going to do?

lost and found

LOST! Small black and white cat with green eyes. Reward. Please telephone 01394 460298.

Lost! Man's watch. Reward. Please telephone 01491 575490 or fax 01491 573590.

Found in High Street. Small grey cat. Very pretty and friendly. Phone 01472 630457.

Prof. English
When people lose things, they usually go to the police station. Sometimes they put an advertisement in a newspaper too. When people find things, they usually take them to the police station, but sometimes they put an advertisement in the newspaper.

a police station

an advertisement

a reward

perhaps

Kit	I feel ill.
Max	Perhaps you've got flu.
Kit	Perhaps I have.
Prof. English	Perhaps Kit has flu, and perhaps she hasn't – we don't **know**.

Charlie's boots

Charlie often loses things. Last week he lost his football boots.

"How did you lose them?" asked his mother.

"I don't know," said Charlie. "I came home from school on the bus. I had the boots when I got on the bus."

His mother thought for a moment, then she said, "Perhaps you left them on the bus."

"Perhaps you're right," said Charlie.

"Telephone the bus station and ask," said his mother. "Perhaps somebody found them."

Charlie telephoned the bus station. "Did anybody find a pair of black and green football boots on the Number 23 bus, please?" he said.

"One moment, please," said the man. He went away for a few minutes, then he came back to the telephone again. "Yes," he said. "Somebody found them and gave them to the driver. They're at the bus station now. Please come and get them."

Charlie walked to the bus station. He told the man his name and address, and the man gave him the football boots. Charlie was tired, so he went home by bus . . . and he left his football boots on the bus again!

Exercise

A Which words are correct? Read the story again and find the correct answer.
Example: *Charlie lost his football boots.*

Charlie lost his tennis shoes/football boots/sunglasses.
He came home from work/school on foot/by train/by bus.
Charlie/his father/his mother visited/telephoned/wrote to
the bus station/airport/railway station.
"Did anybody find a pair of tennis shoes/football boots/
sunglasses in the street/at the railway station/
on the Number 23 bus?" he asked.
The man went away for a long time/for a moment/
for a few minutes.
"Yes," he said, "Someone found them."
Charlie went to the bus station/airport/railway station
by car/by bike/on foot.
He gave the man some money/his name and address/
a letter from his mother and the man gave him
the tennis shoes/football boots/sunglasses . . .
Then Charlie lost them again!

Rosy's wedding dress

Rosy	That's nothing. I once left my wedding dress on a London bus.
Prof. English	Did you find it again?
Rosy	Yes, I did. A bus driver found it. I sent him a piece of wedding cake.

could

Prof. English
The past tense of **can** is **could**.

When I was young I could touch my toes, but I couldn't drive a car.
When I was young I could run very fast, but I couldn't speak German.
When I was young I could dance, but I couldn't play chess.

try to . . .

Kit tried to catch the bird. She could not catch it because she was not fast enough.

Tuna sandwiches

Tim was hungry. He looked in the fridge, but he could not find any food. Then he found a tin of tuna in the cupboard . . . but he could not find a tin-opener. He tried to open the tin with a knife, but he could not, because the knife was not strong enough.

Tim looked at his watch. "It's eight o'clock," he said sadly. "I can't buy any food. The shops closed a long time ago."

He went to Barbara's house and rang the door bell. Barbara came to the door.

"Hello, Tim," she said. She saw the tin of tuna. "Oh Tim," she said, "You've got a present for me."

"Er . . . no, I haven't," said Tim. His face was very red. "It's a tin of tuna. I was hungry and I tried to find some food. I found this tin of tuna, and I tried to open the tin with a knife, but I broke the knife. I couldn't find a tin-opener. I couldn't buy food because all the shops were closed . . . and I'm very hungry. Have you got a tin-opener, please?"

"Oh, Tim! You really are silly sometimes!" said Barbara. "Come in."

Barbara took a tin-opener out of a cupboard. Carefully she opened the tin. She looked at the tuna. "This looks good," she said.

"Would you like some?" asked Tim.

"Yes, please," said Barbara. "Listen . . . I bought some bread this morning. Let's have tuna sandwiches."

"OK," said Tim. He cut the bread and Barbara buttered it. They made a lot of tuna sandwiches and put them on a big plate. Barbara made some tea and they had their supper together.

a tin of tuna

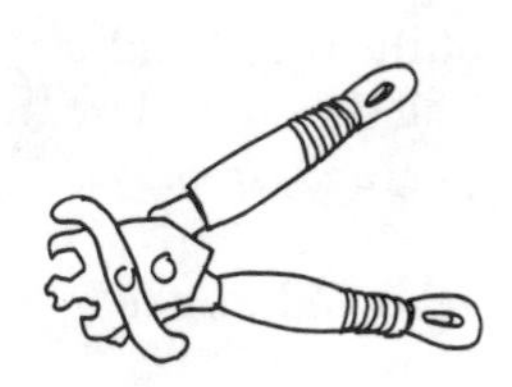

a tin-opener

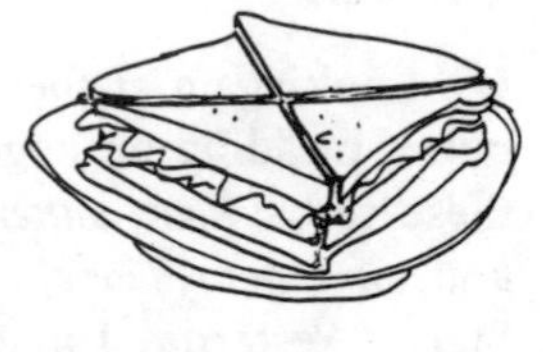

a plate of sandwiches

The first sandwich

Prof. English	Do you know the story of the Earl of Sandwich?
Max	What's an earl?
Prof. English	An important man with a lot of money. Well . . .

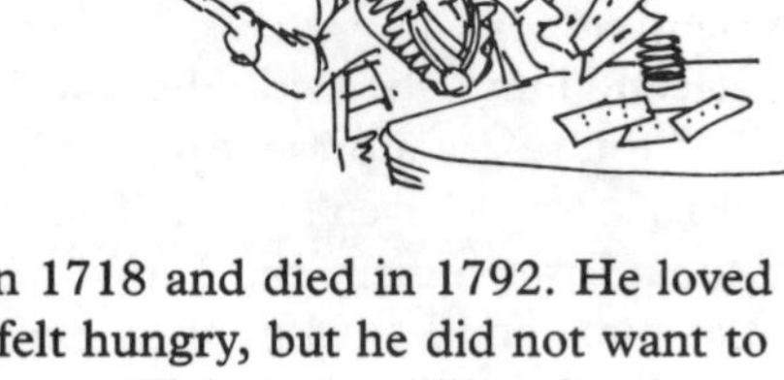

The Earl of Sandwich was born in 1718 and died in 1792. He loved playing cards. One night the earl felt hungry, but he did not want to stop playing. So he said to his servant, "Bring me a slice of meat between two slices of bread."

The servant went to the kitchen and said to the cook: "The Earl wants a slice of meat between two slices of bread."

The cook cut two slices of bread and buttered them. He put a slice of meat between the two slices of bread. He gave this to the servant, and the servant took it to the earl. The earl ate it, liked it and asked for another.

"This is wonderful," he said. "Let's call it a sandwich."
And that is how sandwiches got their name.

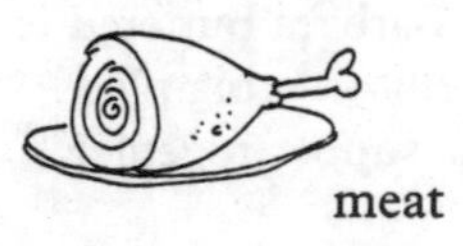

meat

bring

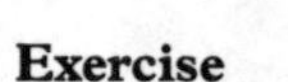

Exercise

B Look again at the story of the bread and butter pudding on page 90. Tell the story. Use these verbs: *heat, butter, cut, put, add, sprinkle, beat, mix, pour, leave, cook.*
Start: "Yesterday I made a bread and butter pudding."
Finish your story with: "I (cook) the bread and butter pudding until it was brown. I (take) it out of the oven. Then I (ask) my best friends to come and we (eat) the pudding. It tasted very nice."

going to

Amy is going to jump into the swimming pool.

She is jumping into the water.

Splash! She is in the water.

Prof. English — *Amy is going to jump* is called the **future continuous** tense. It goes like this:

Write 	**Say** 
I am going to jump. He/She/It is going to jump. You/We/They are going to jump.	I'm going to jump. He/She/It's going to jump. You/We/They're going to jump.
Am I going to jump? Is he/she/it going to jump? Are you/we/they going to jump?	Am I going to jump? Is he/she/it going to jump? Are you/we/they going to jump?
Yes, I am. No, I am not. Yes, he/she/it is. No, he/she/it is not.	Yes, I am. No, I'm not. Yes, he/she/it is. No, he/she/it isn't. / No, he/she/ it's not.
Yes, you/we/they are. No, you/we/they are not.	Yes, you/we/they are. No, you/we/they aren't. / No, you/ we/they're not.
I am not going to jump. He/She/It is not going to jump.	I'm not going to jump. He/She/It's not going to jump. / He/She/It isn't going to jump.
You/We/They are not going to jump.	You/We/They aren't going to jump. / You/We/They're not going to jump.

The cat is going to play the fiddle, and the mouse is going to run away.

Barbara is going to mend her car.

Charlie and James are going to walk to school.

Mr Duncan	I'm going to play in another concert tomorrow.
Barbara	That's wonderful. You played Rossini last week. What are you going to play tomorrow?

Mr Duncan	*Take the A Train.* It's a jazz concert.

soon; in (three days)' time

Max — I'm going to go to a concert soon.
Kit — That's nice. When are you going?
Max — In three days' time.
Kit — Super! Who are you going to go with?
Max — My girlfriend. She's wonderful. She wears beautiful clothes and she always smells nice. We're going to go on holiday together **in a month's time** . . . She's going to come here **soon**.
Kit — When?
Max — What time is it?
Kit — Seven twenty p.m.
Max — Oh! She's going to come here in ten minutes' time! (*The door bell rings.*) And here she is! She's ten minutes early!

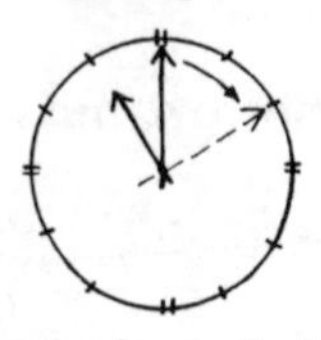

in ten minutes' time

ten minutes early

five minutes late

Exercise

C Look at the pictures and answer the questions.
Example: 1 What is Charlie going to do?
He is going to clean his teeth.

1

2 3

4 5

6

7 8

9 10

1 What is Charlie going to do?
2 Where is Tim going to go?
3 Is Barbara going to mend her car?
4 What is Harry going to do?
5 Is Tim going to write a letter?
6 Is James going to play football?
7 Is Mr Duncan going to play the double bass?
8 Where is Kit going to go?
9 What is Amy going to do?
10 Is Fred going to take Jimmy for a walk?

tomorrow, next week, next month, next year

Prof. English Today's Tuesday. I'm going to buy a new bed on Wednesday. I'm going to buy a new bed in a day's time. I'm going to buy it **tomorrow**.

Kit Today's the fourteenth of June. I'm going to go on holiday on the twenty-first of June. I'm going to go on holiday in a week's time. I'm going to go on holiday **next week**.

Max It's the fourteenth of June, and I'm going to fly to Paris on the fourteenth of July. I'm going to fly to Paris in a month's time. I'm going to fly there **next month**.

Prof. English It's 1997. I'm going to stop drinking wine in 1998. I'm going to stop drinking wine in a year's time. I'm going to stop drinking it **next year**.

a studio

Reporter Good evening, and welcome to *School Story*. There are lots of young people in the studio and I'm going to ask them some questions. Now, Paul, what are you going to do for a living?

Paul I'm going to be an engineer. I'm going to build bridges and roads.

Reporter And what about you, Daisy?

Daisy I'm going to be a pop star. I'm going to make lots of CDs, and I'm going to play in lots of concerts. I'm going to be very, very rich. I'm going to marry a nice young man, and we're going to live together in a big house with a swimming pool.

Reporter Er . . . that's wonderful, Daisy. And what about you, Edward; what are you going to do?

Edward I'm going to marry Daisy!

Prof. English The reporter said, *What are you* ***going to do*** *when you* ***leave*** *school?* That's correct. Kit's going to go to London tomorrow. Kit, what are you going to do there?

Kit I'm going to find a long queue outside a concert hall. I'm going to play music, and people are going to give me money!

Prof. English In the future continuous tense, **all** verbs are **regular**. It's easier than the past tense! You can say *I'm going to work in a restaurant and I'm going to cook wonderful meals.* Or you can make it shorter: you can say *I'm going to work in a restaurant and cook wonderful meals.*

Kit Professor, are you going to tell us another story?

Prof. English Not now, Kit. I'm too busy. Sorry. I'm going to teach you another tense.

Exercise

D Miss Brown is a teacher. Yesterday she asked her students, "What are you going to be?" Read the notes and answer the questions.

Example: 1 *Bill: I'm going to be a doctor. I'm going to help people.*

1 Bill – doctor – help people.
2 Connie – artist – paint beautiful pictures.
3 Tommy – teacher – teach little children the alphabet.
4 Eleanor – engineer – build roads and bridges.
5 Mike – secretary – work in an office.
6 Vicky – film star – make exciting films.
7 Sam – cook – cook wonderful meals for famous people.
8 John – fireman – drive a fire engine.

22 I'm still reading

Charlie has cleaned his teeth

Charlie is going to clean his teeth.

Charlie is cleaning his teeth.

Charlie has cleaned his teeth.

Barbara Look, Tim: Amy and Charlie have cleaned my car.

Tim It looks wonderful. When did they clean it?

Barbara This morning. I was very pleased. I gave them £2.

Prof. English *I have cleaned the car* is the **present perfect tense.** I call it the "finished" tense. It goes like this:

Write	**Say**
I/you/we/they **have cleaned** he/she/it **has cleaned**	I/you/we/they**'ve cleaned** he/she/it**'s cleaned**
have I/you/we/they **cleaned**? **has** he/she/it **cleaned**?	**have** I/you/we/they **cleaned**? **has** he/she/it **cleaned**?
I/you/we/they **have not cleaned**	I/you/we/they **haven't cleaned**

Prof. English Regular verbs in this tense are easy. Here are some examples:

We **have washed** our hair and now we are going to dry it.
The driver **has stopped** the bus, and now the people are getting in.
Charlie and James **have jumped** into the swimming pool, and now they are swimming.
I **have finished** my exercise and now I am going to watch TV.
You **have not polished** the car; it looks very dirty.

Prof. English The irregular verbs are a little more difficult – but here are a few easy ones!

read – read – read: We**'ve read** *Little Women* and we're going to read *Good Wives* next week.
put – put – put: Brenda **has put** the clean clothes into the washing machine, and now they are going round and round.
cut – cut – cut: Barbara **has cut** the bread and now she is going to make sandwiches.
hurt – hurt – hurt:

hit – hit – hit:

Prof. English But we say **beat – beat – beaten**. I've **beaten** the eggs and now I'm going to make an omelette.

Kit Oh, good! What are you going to put in it?

Prof. English Cheese. I love cheese omelettes.

blow – blew – blown: The wind **has blown** Fred's hat off.

lose – lost – lost: Charlie **has lost** his football boots.
find – found – found: Brenda **has found** Charlie's football boots.

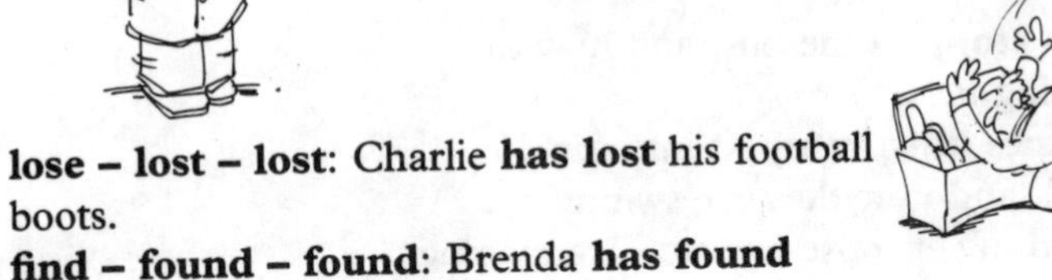

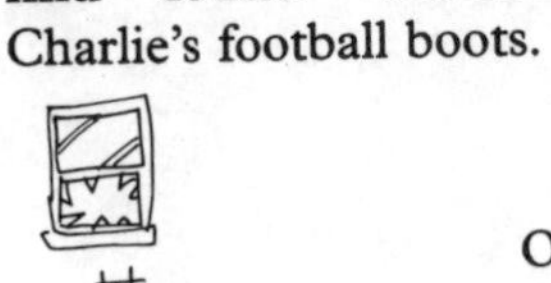

Oh dear! **I've broken** a window.
Tim **has bought** a new car.

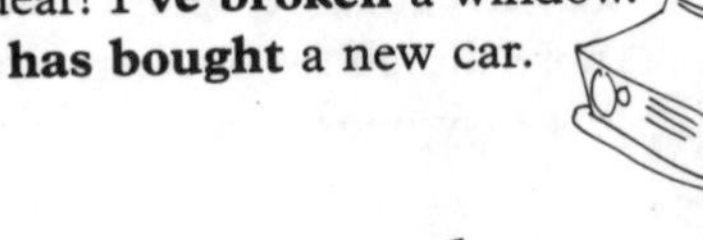

Amy **has brought** a baby rabbit to school.

The engineers **have built** a bridge.

Brenda is worried because the boys **have not come** home from school.

Oh dear! **I've done** something silly!

Be careful, the men **have dug** a big hole in the road.
I **have drawn** a picture of a rabbit.

The boys **have drunk** all the milk and now we haven't any.

We **have driven** through the fog and now we are very tired.
Somebody **has eaten** all the biscuits!

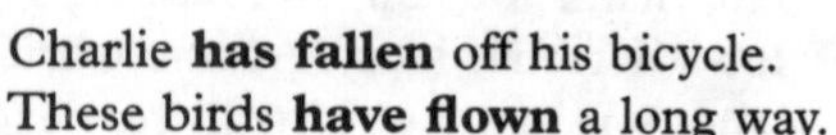

Charlie **has fallen** off his bicycle.
These birds **have flown** a long way.

The pipes **have frozen** and we haven't any water.
Charlie **has got up** early and now he is having his breakfast.
Harry**'s gone** to work. Do you want his telephone number?
Barbara **has given** Tim a new tie.
We **have had** our breakfast.
Bob **has left** the office and is driving home.
Paul Revere **has ridden** a long way with the news.
Somebody **has rung** the bell and Barbara is coming to the door.
I **have run** 500 metres and now I'm going to have a drink.
This is terrible: I**'ve slept** for nine hours and now I'm going to be late for work.
The fat lady **has sung** her song and **sat** down again.
Barbara **has spent** £60 in the clothes shop and now she has no money.
Fred **has taken** Jim for a walk and now they are both tired.
Brenda **has taught** Amy to type, and now Amy can type very fast.
"**Have** you **thought** about buying a new car?"
"Yes, but I haven't enough money."
Tim **has written** a lot of letters and now he is going to post them.
Barbara **has** never **worn** these shoes. They are still new.

Prof. English I **have said** a lot about irregular verbs, and now I am going to teach you something new.

still and just

Max Have you finished reading your book?

Kit I've just finished. I started yesterday and I read the last word a moment ago. Do you want to read it?

Max No, thank you. I'm still reading *The Mousetrap.* It's a detective story. Agatha Christie wrote it a long time ago, but it's still very exciting.

Prof. English **Just** can mean lots of things. *I'm **just** a poor old teacher* means *I'm **only** a poor old teacher. I've* **just** *had my lunch* means *I had my lunch a short time ago.*
We say things like **Just a moment** – that means *Please wait a moment.*
Just now means *now; at this moment* (in the present). **Just then** means *at that moment* (in the past).

Max Professor, would you like a crisp?

Prof. English Not just now, thank you, Max. I'm not hungry. I've just had my lunch.
Still is another useful word. When we say *I'm **still** reading my book,* we mean *I haven't finished it.*

Harry Hello, Brenda. I've just arrived in Karachi. I'm still at the airport.

Brenda Are you all right?

Harry I'm fine, thank you, but I'm very tired. I've been awake for 26 hours. I'm going to go to bed.

Charlie Mum, have you washed my football shirt?

Brenda Just a minute, Charlie, I'm on the telephone.
(to Harry) Goodbye, Harry. Sleep well . . . Charlie!

Charlie Yes, mum.

Brenda I've just spoken to your father. He's just arrived in Karachi. He's going to bed.

Charlie Is he OK?

Brenda Yes, he's fine. He's just very tired. Now, have you found your football shirt?

The cat is on the telephone.

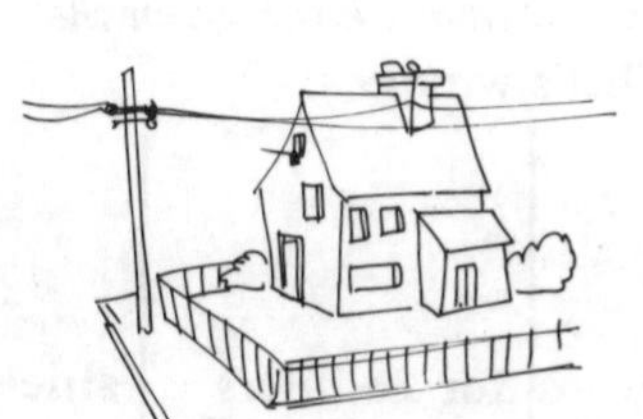

This house is on the telephone.

Brenda is on the telephone.

for and since

Harry is very tired. Today is Monday and it is 8 p.m. He got up at 6 a.m. yesterday. He is still awake. He has been awake **for** 26 hours. He has been awake **since** 6 a.m. yesterday.

Barbara got into the bath at ten past six. She is still in the bath. She has been in the bath **since** ten past six.

Prof. English
You can say *Barbara has been in the bath* ***for*** *35 minutes* or *Barbara has been in the bath* ***since*** *ten past six*. But you can't say *Barbara has been in the bath since 35 minutes*. That's wrong.

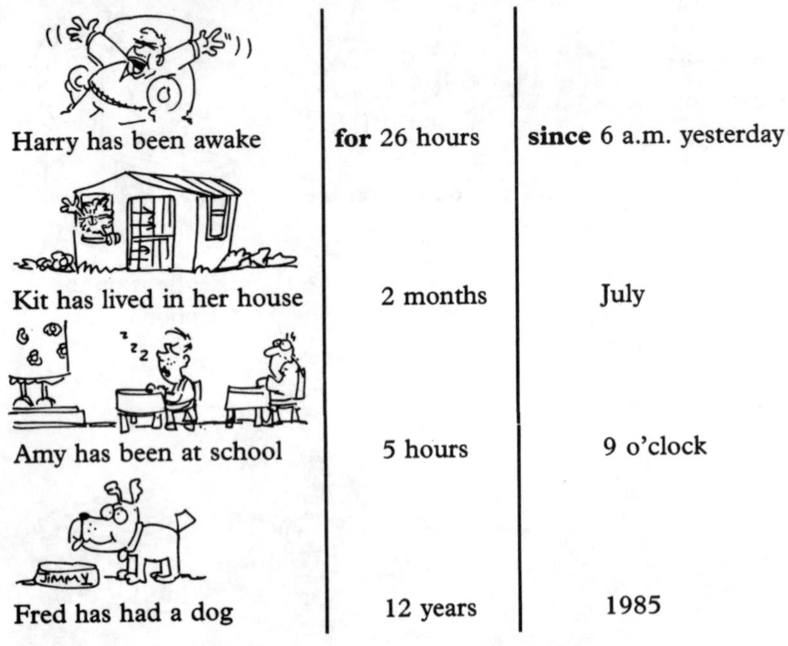

Harry has been awake	**for** 26 hours	**since** 6 a.m. yesterday
Kit has lived in her house	2 months	July
Amy has been at school	5 hours	9 o'clock
Fred has had a dog	12 years	1985

Exercises

A Write sentences. Use *for*.
Example: 1 *Barbara has been in the shower for twenty minutes.*

1 Barbara – in the shower – 20 minutes.
2 Harry – an engineer – a long time.
3 The old man – in hospital – 6 weeks.
4 Amy – in her tree house – 3 hours.
5 Rosy – live in Eyke – 20 years.

B Write sentences. Use *since*.
Example: 1 *Harry has been in the garden since 2 o'clock.*

1 Harry – in the garden – 2 o'clock.
2 Brenda – secretary – 1982.
3 Tim – work in an office – the age of 18.
4 Fred – have Jimmy – 1985.
5 Max – asleep – 3 a.m.

already and yet

Teacher Good boy, Andy. You've finished your sums already. Colin is still doing his, and Amy hasn't started hers yet.
Why are you crying, Joe?

Joe My dad's given me a book for my birthday, but I've already got one!

2000 → ?

Prof. English
Look at this time line. I am pointing to **now**. Some things have **already** happened, and some things haven't happened **yet**. And some things are **still** happening: Rosy was **already** married to John in 1972. She is **still** married. She hasn't left John **yet**!

I have been . . . ing

Prof. English I've been teaching English for a long time.

Kit How long have you been teaching, Professor?

Prof. English Well, I started teaching when I was 23. I've been teaching since I was 23. I'm nearly 50 now and I'm still teaching, so I've been teaching English for nearly 27 years.

Kit That's a long time.

Man The bus is late. I've been waiting here for twenty minutes.

Woman Yes, the bus is very late. I've been standing here since half past two.

Exercises

C Use these notes to help you to write sentences. Use *has/have been* and either *since* or *for.*

Examples: 1 *Fred's dog has been ill for two days.*
2 *Charlie has been asleep since 10 o'clock.*

1 Fred's dog – be ill – two days.
2 Charlie – be asleep – 10 o'clock.
3 Mary and Jack – be married – 21 years.
4 Paul and Sarah – be married – 1989.
5 Amy – be at home – 4 o'clock.
6 James – be at school – three hours.
7 Max and Kit – be in the kitchen – this afternoon.
8 Professor English – be awake – 5 a.m.
9 Brenda and Harry – live in this house – 12 years.
10 Della – have this job – 1992.
11 Tim – be in the bath – 10 minutes.
12 Barbara – be in the shower – 6 o'clock.

D Write sentences using these notes. Use *has/have been . . . ing* and either *since* or *for.*

Examples: 1 *We have been working here for 12 years.*
2 *Barbara has been painting her fingernails since 5 o'clock.*

1 We – work here – 12 years.
2 Barbara – paint her fingernails – 5 o'clock.
3 Harry – wait for Brenda – 20 minutes.
4 Kit – play the fiddle – two hours.
5 Max and Kit – cook – 2 o'clock.
6 Charlie – read a book – half an hour.
7 Brenda – clean the kitchen – 12 o'clock.
8 Fred – play with his dog – an hour and a half.
9 It – rain – Tuesday morning.
10 It – snow – three hours.

E Look at the pictures and answer the questions.

Example: 1 Has Barbara got up yet? *No, she has not.*

1 Has Barbara got up yet?
2 Is she still in bed?
3 Has Mr Duncan telephoned yet?
4 Is Barbara still talking to him?
5 Has Barbara finished writing Mr Duncan's address yet?

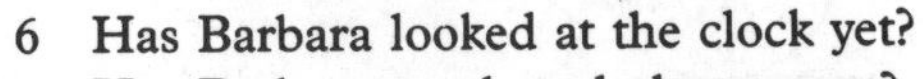

6 Has Barbara looked at the clock yet?
7 Has Barbara put her clothes on yet?

8 Has Barbara had her shower yet?
9 Is she still in the shower?
10 Has Barbara arrived at Mr Duncan's house yet?
11 Is she still driving to his house?
12 Has Barbara met Mr Duncan yet?

F Write in the spaces.

Example: Prof. English: Please read page 120.
You: *I've already read it.*

Prof. English: Please read page 120.
You: ....
Prof. English: Please do the exercises on page 188.
You: ....
Prof. English: OK. That's very good. Please read the story of Puss in Boots.
You: ....
Prof. English: Fine! Have you read the story of the Town Mouse and the Country Mouse too?
You: ....

23 Have you ever . . . ?

before and after

Look at the time line. Look at 1900. Lots of things happened **before** 1900. And lots of things happened **after** 1900. What is going to happen in 2010?

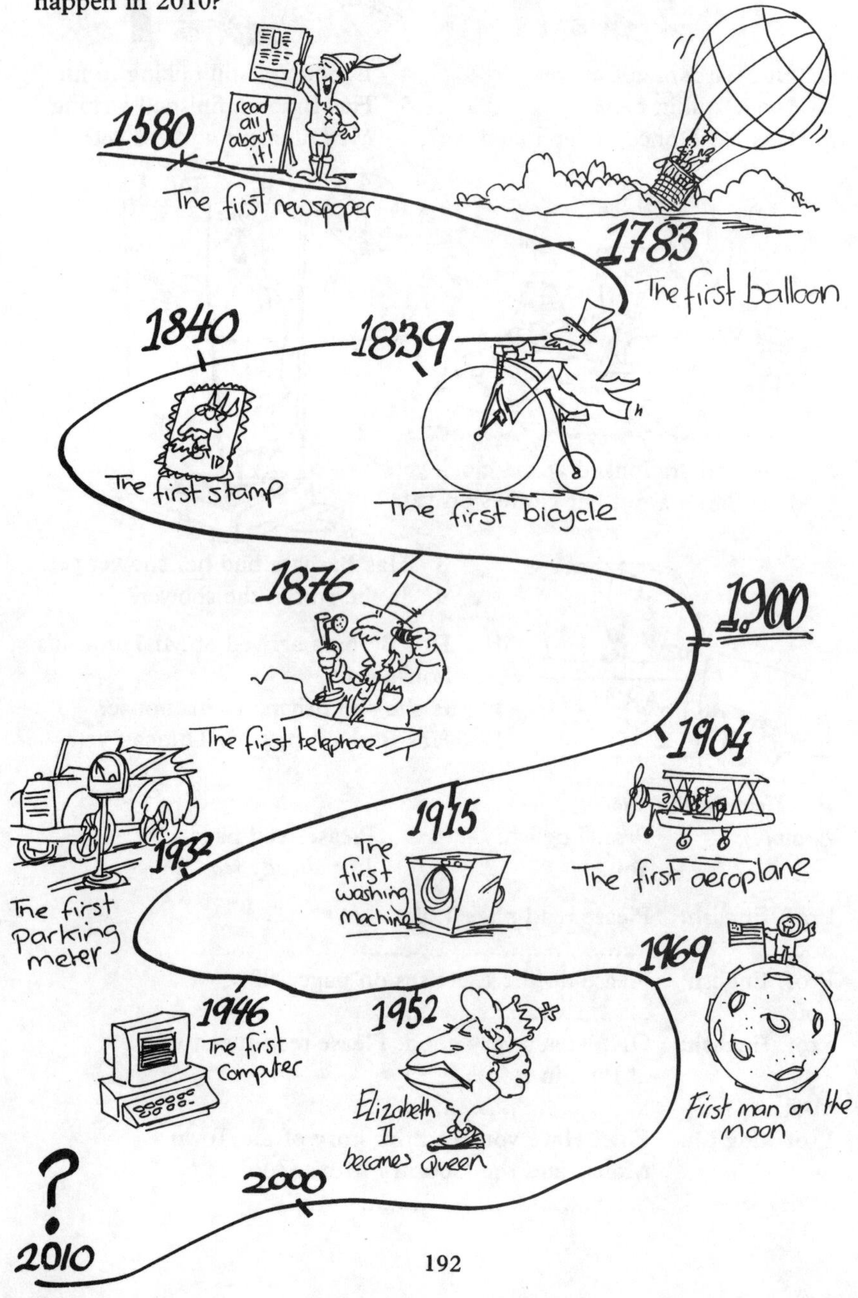

Past, present and future

Prof. English	Look at the time line again. We call the time before NOW **the past**. We call NOW **the present**. And the time after NOW is **the future**.
Max	I often think about the future. Am I going to be famous?
Kit	Perhaps you are. I'm famous enough already. There's a song about me. It's called *The Cat and the Fiddle*. There's a story about me. It's called *Puss in Boots*. Nobody's written a story about a mouse yet.
Prof. English	Kit, you're wrong. There are lots of stories about mice, and I'm going to tell you one. It's called *The Town Mouse and the Country Mouse*.

The Town Mouse and the Country Mouse

A lot of people live happily in the town; and a lot of people like living in the country. But the country is very different from the town, and country people and town people live very different lives. "Different" does not mean better, and it does not mean worse – it just means different!

Well, once upon a time there were two mice. The first mouse was a town mouse. He lived in a hole in a big building in the middle of the town, and his name was Mike. The second mouse lived in the country. He lived in a hole in a big old tree, and his name was Matt. Now Matt did not travel very much, but Mike often visited him.

"My friend," said Mike one day, "You need a holiday. Come and spend a few days with me in town. I've got a beautiful hole under the kitchen of a big hotel. It's always warm and dry, and the food's wonderful."

"All right," said Matt.

The streets were full of cars and buses, taxis and bicycles. They all went very fast and made a lot of noise. Matt stood in the middle of the road and looked at the tall, beautiful buildings – and a car nearly hit him.

"What was that?" asked Matt. "It nearly hit me!"

"That was only a car," said Mike.

They went through a lot of tunnels under walls and floors, and after a long time they came to Mike's hole.

Mike said to Matt, "Are you hungry?"

"Oh, yes!" said Matt. "I'm tired too. We've been walking for a long time. My feet hurt."

"Well, let's have dinner!"

The two mice went through another tunnel. Matt looked round. They were in a kitchen. There was a big table in the middle of the kitchen. "Come on," said Mike, and together they climbed up the table leg.

There was a lot of food on the table. It smelt wonderful. Together Mike and Matt picked up a piece of chicken and started to carry it down the table leg and across the floor. Then the door opened and a tall man with a white hat came into the kitchen. He saw the two mice.

"What's happening?" he shouted. He picked up a knife and chased the two mice.

"Who was that?" asked Matt. "He nearly caught us!"

"That was only the cook," said Mike. "He's been trying to catch me for a long time, but I'm too fast for him. Come on, let's eat this chicken."

They finished the chicken. "Let's have some cake," said Mike. He licked his lips. "I'm still hungry. Come on – the cook's gone home and the kitchen's empty."

Very quietly they climbed up the table leg again. They took a big piece of cake and they started to carry it to their hole.

Then Matt saw a big black animal in front of their hole. It looked at them with its big green eyes, and it licked its lips. The two mice left their cake and ran. The cat jumped up and chased them. The mice ran under the fridge. The cat could not touch them, because it was too big. It looked at them angrily with its green eyes and waved its long black tail. Then somebody shouted, "Puss, Puss! Dinner time!" and the cat walked slowly away.

"What was that?" asked Matt.

"It was only a cat," said Mike. "She lives here. She's been trying to catch me for months, but I'm too fast for her. Come on. We haven't had our cake yet!"

The two mice ran under the fridge. Matt saw a piece of cheese. He touched it – and a door closed with a bang and nearly cut his head off.

"What was that?" he asked Mike.

"It's only a mousetrap. The cook sometimes puts mousetraps under the fridge, but he can't catch me. Come on, we haven't had any cake yet!"

"No, thank you," said the little country mouse. "I've seen enough. I don't like living in town, and I want to go home!"

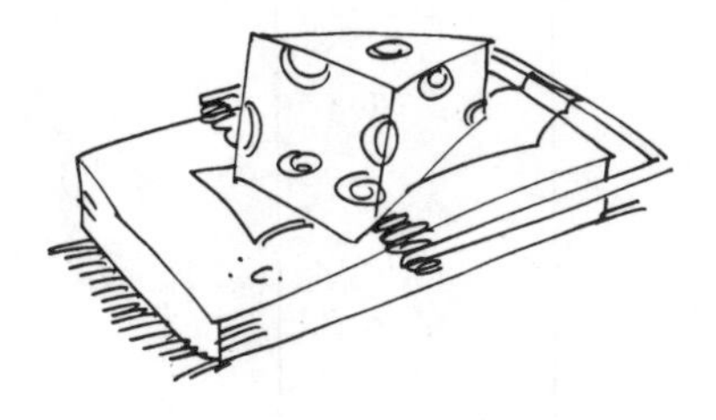

a mousetrap

lick

have gone, have been

Prof. English
The present perfect of **I go** can be **I have gone** or **I have been**.
Harry is not at home. He **has gone** to London. He is building some new offices there. (He is in London now.)
Harry **has been** to Paris lots of times, but he **has** never **been** to Tokyo. (He is not in Paris now.)

Prof. English	Have you ever been to London, Max?
Max	Yes, I have. I've been to London lots of times, but I don't want to live there. It's too noisy and busy. I'm like Matt. I'm a country mouse.
Prof. English	What about you, Kit? Have you ever been to London?
Kit	No, I haven't. I've never been to London. I don't like big towns.
Prof. English	We say **ever** in questions. We say **never** when the answer is *No.* Now you try! Have you ever . . .

	Never	**A few times**	**Lots of times**
swum in the sea?			
drunk champagne?			
eaten cherries?			
broken an expensive dish?			
seen a rainbow?			
played the violin?			
fallen into a swimming pool?			
dug a hole?			
lost a lot of money?			
won a game of chess?			
danced with a famous film star?			
been through a tunnel?			
taught a cat to talk?			

Prof. English Well, we've finished the book.

Max Yes. And now Kit's going to sing her song. Go on, Kit. You've been waiting a long time for this moment.

Kit OK!

Hey diddle diddle, the cat and the fiddle,
The cow jumped over the moon.
The little dog laughed to see such fun,
And the dish ran away with the spoon.

Answers to exercises

1 Hello!

A a ewe; an apricot; a name; a day; a cherry; an artist; a kitten; a cucumber; a dentist; a fax; a hat; an umbrella; an hour; a mouth; an iguana; a year; an author; a uvula; a queue; an ice cream; an ear; a rabbit; a sheep; an apple

B dentist; ice cream; circle; thirteen; queue; gnome; umbrella; orange; water; address; xylophone; chalet

C hat; fax; potato; van; lips; egg; mouse; circle; queue; dog; book; gate; orange; thirteen; zebra; teeth

D 1 × 2 ✓ 3 × 4 ✓ 5 × 6 × 7 ✓ 8 × 9 ✓ 10 ×

E Rosy: Good morning, Professor. How are you?
Prof. English: I'm very well, thank you, Rosy. How are you?
Rosy: I'm fine thanks/thank you.

2 Names and numbers

C three apricots; twelve cherries; five oranges

D four; one; seventeen; nine; twenty; a hundred and fifty-five; forty-two; a hundred; a hundred and eighty-four; sixty-eight; seventy-six; eighty-eight; two hundred and twenty; four hundred and thirty-one; seven hundred and nine

E 58; 1,203; 61; 124; 809; 9,000,000; 4; 90; 10,000,000,000; 27

F O (or nought, or zero) one four seven three, two double five double eight
O (or nought, or zero) one seven one, four double O, four two four
O (or nought, or zero) one seven two, eight three two eight three two
O (or nought, or zero) one eight one, eight nine two, double three five

3 This and that

A 1 These are birds. 2 This is an ice cream. 3 That is a boat. 4 Those are apple trees. 5 Are these rabbits? 6 Is this an aeroplane? 7 Are those kittens? 8 Is that a passport? 9 What's this? It's a cat. 10 What's that? It's a sheep. 11 What are these? They're boats. 12 What are those? They're gates.

B 1 Who's this? 2 What's this? 3 What are these? 4 Who's this? 5 What's this? 6 What are these? 7 What's this? 8 Who's this? 9 What are these? 10 What's this? 11 What are these? 12 Who's this?

C 1 Is Brenda a doctor? No, she is not. She is a secretary. 2 Is Harry a secretary? No, he is not. He is an engineer. 3 Are Sandy and Paul doctors? No, they are not. They are police officers. 4 Are Della and

Andy police officers? No, they are not. They are doctors. 5 Is Professor English a reporter? No, he is not. He is a teacher. 6 Is Max Mouse a writer? No, he is not. He is a reporter. 7 Are Timm Joy and David Hockney writers? No, they are not. They are artists. 8 Is Rosy Border an artist? No, she is not. She is a writer. 9 Is John a teacher? No, he is not. He is a fireman.

D 1 Is Brenda a secretary? Yes, she is. 2 Are Della and Andy doctors? Yes, they are. 3 Is Shakespeare a writer? Yes, he is. 4 Are Sandy and Paul police officers? Yes, they are. 5 Is John a fireman? Yes, he is. 6 Is Timm Joy an artist? Yes, he is. 7 Are Diego Maradona and Eric Cantona footballers? Yes, they are. 8 Is Paul a police officer? Yes, he is.

E 1 This is Paul Newman. He is a film star. 2 This is Isambard Kingdom Brunel. He is an engineer. 3 This is Madonna. She is a singer. 4 This is Diego Maradona. He is a footballer. 5 This is George Eliot. She is an author. 6 This is Marie Curie. She is a scientist. 7 This is Wolfgang Amadeus Mozart. He is a composer. 8 This is Leonardo da Vinci. He is an artist. 9 This is Socrates. He is a teacher.

F 1 firemen 2 ladies 3 teeth 4 sheep 5 babies 6 tomatoes 7 firemen 8 chemists 9 cherries 10 feet 11 mice 12 chalets 13 faxes 14 letters 15 people 16 children 17 knives 18 secretaries 19 potatoes 20 police officers

4 The Williams family

A Professor English's address; the policemen's cars; the dog's nose; Harry's children; Max's mother; my two sons' names; Barbara's boyfriend's car; the three pterodactyls' tails.

B
1 Have you got a car, Max? No, I haven't.
2 Has James got a brother? Yes, he has.
3 Has Professor English got an aeroplane? No, he has not.
4 Have Kit and Max got tails? Yes, they have.

C 1 Charlie, have you got your books? 2 This is Barbara and this is her taxi. 3 These are dogs and these are their tails. 4 Has Harry got his hat? Yes, he has. 5 I am a doctor and my name is Della. 6 This is a mouse and this is its nose.

D yours; his; theirs; mine; Harry's; ours; Tim's; yours; mine; hers

5 Speaking and writing

A 1 Who's this? It's Brenda. 2 Whose is this? It's Tim's. 3 Whose is this? It's ours. 4 Who's this? It's Professor English. 5 Whose is this? It's theirs. 6 Who's this? It's Max. 7 Whose is this? It's hers. 8 Whose is this? It's his. 9 Who's this? It's Harry.

B There are six people in the Williams family. Their names are Harry Williams, Brenda Williams, Barbara Williams, James Williams, Charlie

Williams and Amy Williams. Harry is 49. Brenda is 45. Barbara is 23. James is 17. Charlie is 14. Amy is 10.

E 1 She is buying a hat. 2 He is singing. 3 She is crying. 4 She is laughing. 5 He is talking. 6 Max is standing in the rain./It is raining. 7 He is reading a book. 8 She is drinking. 9 He is standing. 10 She is washing. 11 He is thinking. 12 She is eating an apple.

6 The time and the weather

A 1 Barbara is wearing her coat. The weather is cold. 2 Tim is wearing his sunglasses. The weather is sunny. 3 Brenda has got her umbrella. The weather is wet. 4 Charlie and James are wearing their swimming trunks. The weather is hot. 5 Harry is wearing his big boots. The weather is snowy.

B 1 It is (a) quarter past two. 2 It is (a) quarter to eight. 3 It is twenty-five (minutes) to ten. 4 It is eleven minutes past ten. 5 It is half past twelve. 6 It is twelve minutes past one. 7 It is thirteen minutes to nine. 8 It is five (minutes) to five. 9 It is ten (minutes) to seven. 10 It is five (minutes) past eleven.

C 1 It is half past six in the evening. The temperature is fifteen degrees and the weather is foggy. (*or* It is foggy) 2 It is twenty past seven in the morning. The temperature is thirty degrees and the weather is hot and sunny. (*or* It is hot and sunny) 3 It is half past two in the afternoon. The temperature is four degrees and the weather is snowy. (*or* It is snowy) 4 It is twenty past eleven in the morning. The temperature is nine degrees and the weather is very windy. (*or* It is very windy) 5 It is quarter past ten in the evening. The temperature is twelve degrees and the weather is cloudy. (*or* It is cloudy) 6 It is quarter to five in the afternoon (evening). The temperature is thirteen degrees and it is raining. (*or* The weather is rainy) 7 It is quarter to twelve in the morning. The temperature is twenty-two degrees and the weather is dry, hot and cloudy. (*or* It is dry, hot and cloudy) 8 It is twelve minutes past one in the afternoon. The temperature is nought degrees. It is freezing.

7 What are you wearing?

A 1 Max is putting his boots on. 2 Kit is taking her hat off. 3 Barbara is taking her dress off. 4 Tim is putting his shoes on. 5 Professor English is taking his shirt off. 6 Tim and Barbara are putting their T-shirts on. 7 We are taking our socks off. 8 You are putting your tie on. 9 The firemen are taking their helmets off. 10 I am putting my coat on.

B 1 Tim is saying, "Hello, Barbara, how are you?" Barbara is saying, "I'm fine, thanks. How are you?" 2 "Whose trousers are those? Are they yours, Kit?" "No, they aren't mine, they're Max's." 3 Mr Duncan is telephoning Barbara. Barbara is in the shower. 4 Hello, Kit. What's the weather like? What's the temperature? Are you wearing your boots?

C 1 Tim is looking at an aeroplane. 2 Barbara and Tim are watching TV. 3 Amy is listening to a bird. 4 Charlie is not listening to the teacher. He is listening to his radio. 5 The people are watching a film. 6 Brenda is looking at the children's dirty clothes. 7 James is listening to music.

D *Examples:* 1 A is looking at the teacher/listening to the radio. 2 B is writing/listening to the teacher. 3 Yes, C is listening to the teacher and watching the teacher. 4 The teacher is saying, "Are you listening?" 5 D is thinking, "You're boring!"

8 Don't stop!

A 1 The mice are running away because the cat is chasing them. 2 The mice are saying "He's chasing us!" 3 Barbara has got an apple. Tim is saying "Don't eat it!" 4 Joe is crying because Amy is hitting him. 5 Harry is saying "I'm mending the lamp", and James is saying "I'm helping you." 6 Tim is helping Barbara. He is helping her. 7 The children are playing and their mother is looking at them.

B 1 Don't play football in the house, Charlie. 2 Don't ride your bicycle on the grass, Amy. 3 Don't pick the flowers, Joe. 4 Don't jump on the bed, Amy. 5 Don't sing in the shower, Barbara. 6 Don't park on the grass, Tim. 7 Don't smoke in bed, Tim. 8 Don't pull the cat's tail.

C 1 Stop playing the fiddle, Kit. 2 Stop singing, Max. 3 Stop playing football, Joe. 4 Stop picking the flowers, Amy. 5 Stop pulling the dog's tail. 6 Stop eating chocolates, Brenda. 7 Stop pulling the dog's ears. 8 Stop eating the flowers. 9 Stop reading James's letter, Charlie.

D 1 It's May the twenty-fifth./It's the twenty-fifth of May. 2 It's March the twenty-first./It's the twenty-first of March. 3 It's September the thirtieth./It's the thirtieth of September. 4 It's June the first./It's the first of June. 5 It's October the thirty-first./It's the thirty-first of October. 6 It's January the seventeenth./It's the seventeenth of January. 7 It's July the second./It's the second of July. 8 It's April the tenth./It's the tenth of April.

E 1 My birthday is on November the twenty-seventh. It's on the twenty-seventh of November. 2 My birthday is on February the nineteenth. It's on the nineteenth of February. 3 My birthday is on August the first. It's on the first of August. 4 My birthday is on December the twenty-third. It's on the twenty-third of December. 5 My birthday is on March the seventeenth. It's on the seventeenth of March. 6 My birthday is on December the thirty-first. It's on the thirty-first of December. 7 My birthday is on July the tenth. It's on the tenth of July. 8 My birthday is on June the eighteenth. It's on the eighteenth of June.

F 1 Good morning! It's 8.30 a.m. on Monday the twenty-fifth of August, and it's raining. 2 Good morning! It's 9.32 a.m. on Friday the twenty-fifth of May, and it's sunny. 3 Good afternoon! It's 12.45 p.m. on Tuesday the thirtieth of December, and it's snowing. 4 Good evening! It's 6 p.m. on Wednesday the twenty-eighth of November and it's foggy. 5 Good morning! It's 12 noon on Saturday the twelfth of April, and it's cloudy. 6 Good afternoon! It's 5.15 p.m. on Sunday the twenty-first of March, and it's windy.

G 1 Give it to him. Give him it. 2 Give it to her. Give her it. 3 Send them to her. Send her them. 4 Give them to them. (Give them them.) 5 Give them to us. Give us them.

9 The Williams family at home

A 1 Put the table in the dining room. 2 Put the armchair in the sitting room. 3 Put the sofa in the sitting room. 4 Put the cooker in the kitchen. 5 Put the bath in the bathroom. 6 Put the cupboard in Harry and Brenda's bedroom. 7 Put Amy's bed in Amy's bedroom 8 Put Charlie's bed in Charlie's bedroom. 9 Put James's chest of drawers in James's bedroom. 10 Put the table in the kitchen. 11 Put the chair in the kitchen. 12 Put the wash basin in the downstairs lavatory. 13 Put the towels in the bathroom. 14 Put the dressing table in Harry and Brenda's bedroom.

B 1 Let's watch TV. No, let's play football. 2 Let's have a drink. No, let's play chess. 3 Let's listen to the radio. No, let's play cards. 4 Let's have dinner. No, let's dance. 5 Let's dig the garden. No, let's play the xylophone. 6 Let's wash the car. No, let's drink champagne.

C

D 1 These are football boots. They are Charlie's. 2 These are CDs. They are James's. 3 This is a bed. It is Amy's. 4 This is a dressing table. It is Brenda's. 5 This is a chest of drawers. It is James's.

10 What colour is it?

A 1 Brenda is sitting in front of Charlie. 2 Brenda is sitting beside Harry. 3 Harry is in the driver's seat. 4 She is talking. 5 No, he is not. 6 Amy is sitting between James and Charlie. 7 He is driving. 8 He is wearing a hat.

B *Example:* There are two boys in front of the village sign. They are playing football. There are two women outside the shop. They are talking. There are two people inside the shop. A child is going into the shop. Two men are going into the pub and another man is coming out of the pub. A boy is sitting under a tree. He is reading. A cat is climbing the tree. There are four children on the village green. An old man is sitting on a bench. A woman is getting into the bus. The bus driver is sitting in the driver's seat.

C 1 Red 2 – 3 – 4 Orange 5 White 6 Blue 7 Grey 8 Green 9 Brown/Red/Orange/Yellow 10 Black and white 11 Yellow

D 1 Barbara is making a cheese omelette. 2 James and Charlie are making cheese on toast. 3 Brenda is making a cherry cake. 4 Rosy is making an apple pie.

11 What do you do?

A 1 Charlie reads adventure stories. 2 We have breakfast at seven o'clock. 3 The students have lunch at 12 noon. 4 Brenda watches television on Sunday evenings. 5 My brothers go to the cinema on Saturdays. 6 My mother has tea at four o'clock. 7 Bob starts work at nine o'clock and finishes work at five thirty. 8 Tim drinks coffee in the morning. 9 Doctors help people. 10 Barbara drives a taxi. 11 Bus drivers drive buses. 12 Authors write books and plays.

C 1 I'm a driver. 2 I'm a footballer. 3 I'm a painter. 4 I'm a builder. 5 I'm a runner. 6 I'm a writer. 7 I'm a singer. 8 I'm a dancer. 9 I'm a jumper. 10 I'm a teacher.

12 Always interesting

A 1 The opposite of a cold day is a hot day. 2 The opposite of dry shoes is wet shoes. 3 The opposite of a small cat is a big cat. 4 The opposite of a short man is a tall man. 5 The opposite of a short skirt is a long skirt. 6 The opposite of a long queue of people is a short queue of people. 7 The opposite of a beautiful animal is an ugly animal. 8 The opposite of an interesting story is a boring story. 9 The opposite of a thin cat is a fat cat. 10 The opposite of a cloudy day is a sunny day. 11 The opposite of long trousers is short trousers. 12 The opposite of a fat person is a thin person. 13 The opposite of new clothes is old clothes. 14 The opposite of an old woman is a young woman. 15 The opposite of a good apple is a bad apple.

B 1 (√) 2 (×) 3 (×) 4 (√) 5 (√) 6 (×) 7 (×) 8 (×) 9 (√) 10 (×)

C 1 I always have toast and coffee for breakfast. 2 I usually read horror stories in the evenings. 3 I nearly always have lunch at 1 p.m. 4 I nearly always wear shoes. 5 I hardly ever wear a hat. 6 I often sing in the shower. 7 I hardly ever go to work by taxi. 8 I hardly ever take an umbrella to work. 9 I sometimes listen to opera. 10 I never wear lipstick. 11 I sometimes have a snack in the middle of the afternoon. 12 I never drink champagne.

13 Work and hobbies

A 2 Reporter: What's your hobby?
Me: My hobby is playing the guitar.
Reporter: How often do you play?
Me: I play every day/twice a week (etc.).

3 Reporter: What's your hobby?
Me: My hobby is playing the piano.
Reporter: How often do you play?
Me: I play every day/nearly every day (etc.).

4 Reporter: What's your hobby?
Me: My hobby is cooking.
Reporter: How often do you cook?
Me: I cook . . .

5 Reporter: What's your hobby?
Me: My hobby is watching TV.
Reporter: How often do you watch TV?
Me: I watch TV . . .

6 Reporter: What's your hobby?
Me: My hobby is playing computer games.
Reporter: How often do you play?
Me: I play . . .

7 Reporter: What's your hobby?
Me: My hobby is going fishing.
Reporter: How often do you go fishing?
Me: I go fishing . . .

8 Reporter: What's your hobby?
Me: My hobby is riding.
Reporter: How often do you go riding?
Me: I go riding . . .

9 Reporter: What's your hobby?
Me: My hobby is going to the cinema.
Reporter: How often do you go?
Me: I go . . .

10 Reporter: What's your hobby?
Me: My hobby is going to the pub.
Reporter: How often do you go to the pub?
Me: I go . . .

11 Reporter: What's your hobby?
Me: My hobby is going to parties.
Reporter: How often do you go to parties?
Me: I go . . .

12 Reporter: What's your hobby?
Me: My hobby is going to concerts.
Reporter: How often do you go?
Me: I go . . .

13 Reporter: What's your hobby?
Me: My hobby is reading.
Reporter: How often do you read?

Me: I read . . .

14 Reporter: What's your hobby?
Me: My hobby is painting.
Reporter: How often do you paint?
Me: I paint . . .

B 1 Pavarotti sings beautifully. 2 The old woman walks very slowly. 3 Barbara drives very fast. 4 Charlie plays his CDs very noisily. 5 Brenda usually talks quietly. 6 I eat my breakfast quickly. 7 Barbara cooks very well. 8 Amy paints very nicely.

C 1 He sometimes buys her flowers. 2 He is selling him a bike. 3 She often sends them presents. 4 He is giving her a kiss. 5 He often buys them sweets. 6 He is selling them a cake.

D 2 Me: I'd like a T-shirt, please.
Shopkeeper: What colour would you like?
Me: Red, please.
Shopkeeper: Here you are. That's seven pounds ninety-five pence, please.
Me: Here's ten pounds.
Shopkeeper: And here's two pounds five pence change. Thank you very much.

3 Me: I'd like a pair of socks, please.
Shopkeeper: What colour would you like?
Me: Black and white, please.
Shopkeeper: Here you are. That's two pounds twenty-five pence, please.
Me: Here's three pounds.
Shopkeeper: And here's seventy-five pence change. Thank you very much.

4 Me: I'd like a hat, please.
Shopkeeper: What colour would you like?
Me: Purple, please.
Shopkeeper: Here you are. That's twelve pounds fifty pence, please.
Me: Here's twenty pounds.
Shopkeeper: And here's seven pounds fifty pence change. Thank you very much.

5 Me: I'd like a bag, please.
Shopkeeper: What colour would you like?
Me: Brown, please.
Shopkeeper: Here you are. That's twenty-four pounds ninety-nine pence, please.
Me: Here's twenty-five pounds.
Shopkeeper: And here's a penny change. Thank you very much.

6 Me: I'd like six plates please.
Shopkeeper: What colour would you like?
Me: Red and yellow, please.
Shopkeeper: Here you are. That's twelve pounds thirty pence, please.

Me: Here's fifteen pounds.
Shopkeeper: And here's two pounds seventy pence change. Thank you very much.

14 The biggest and the best

A 1 Me: Good morning. A carton of 12 eggs, please.
Shopkeeper: £1.20, please.
Me: Here's £2.
Shopkeeper. And here's 80p change. Thank you very much.
2 Me: Good morning. A jar of jam, please.
Shopkeeper: 72p, please.
Me: Here's £1.
Shopkeeper: And here's 28p change. Thank you very much.
3 Me: Good morning. A packet of butter, please.
Shopkeeper: 80p, please.
Me: Here's £1.
Shopkeeper. And here's 20p change. Thank you very much.
4 Me: Good morning. 500 grams of cheese, please.
Shopkeeper: £2.25, please.
Me: Here's £2.50.
Shopkeeper. And here's 25p change. Thank you very much.
5 Me: Good morning. A bottle of champagne, please.
Shopkeeper: £22, please.
Me: Here's £25.
Shopkeeper. And here's £3 change. Thank you very much.
6 Me: Good morning. A loaf of bread, please.
Shopkeeper: 43p, please.
Me: Here's 50p.
Shopkeeper. And here's 7p change. Thank you very much.
7 Me: Good morning. A kilo of tomatoes, please.
Shopkeeper: 92p, please.
Me: Here's £1.
Shopkeeper. And here's 8p change. Thank you very much.
8 Me: Good morning. 500 grams of cherries, please.
Shopkeeper: £1.20, please.
Me: Here's £5.
Shopkeeper. And here's £3.80p change. Thank you very much.

B *Examples:*
A toothbrush is cheaper in Britain than it is in France./A toothbrush is more expensive in Britain than it is in the USA.
A pair of shoes is cheaper in France than it is in the USA./A pair of shoes is more expensive in Japan than it is in Britain.

15 What do you want?

B 1 I want an ice cream. 2 I want a car. 3 I want a dress. 4 I want a pair of sunglasses. 5 I want a bicycle. 6 I want a bottle of milk.

C 1 The car needs a wheel. 2 The man needs a pair of shoes. 3 The bus needs a driver. 4 The woman needs a bag. 5 Kit needs a calculator.

D Barbara doesn't want to clean the car. She wants to go shopping.
Tim doesn't want to watch TV. He wants to write letters.
Amy doesn't want to go to the dentist. She wants to play tennis.
Harry doesn't want to mend Charlie's bicycle. He wants to work in the garden.
Brenda doesn't want to go to London. She wants to go to Paris.
James doesn't want to play chess. He wants to listen to music.

16 I'd love one!

A

B 1 The one on the right. 2 The one in the middle. 3 The one on the right. 4 The one on the left. 5 The one on the left. 6 The one in the middle. 7 The one in the middle. 8 The one on the left. 9 The one on the right.

C There are some apples. There is some wine. There is some sugar. There is some tea. There is some coffee. There are some eggs. There is a cucumber. There is a banana. There is some banana. There is a cabbage. There is some cabbage.

D How many apples are there? How much wine is there? How much sugar is there? How much tea is there? How much coffee is there? How many eggs are there? How many cucumbers are there? How many bananas are there? How much banana is there? How many cabbages are there? How much cabbage is there?

17 Everyone has a birthday

A 1 Yes, there is some wine. 2 No, there is no milk. 3 No, there are no cherries. 4 Yes, there is a cucumber. 5 Yes, there is some sugar. 6 Yes, there are some apples. 7 Yes, there are some eggs. 8 No, there is no flour. 9 Yes, there is some cabbage. 10 Yes, there is a cabbage. 11 No, there is no champagne. 12 No, there is no cake.

B There are a lot of eggs but there is only one cucumber. There are a lot of apples but there is only one banana. There are some slices of banana (or There is some banana). There is some tea, and there is some coffee too. There is a cabbage. There is some cabbage. There is some wine, and there is a lot of sugar.

C 1 Yes, there is. There are some eggs/There is a carton of eggs on the top shelf. 2 No, there is not. There is nothing on the second shelf.
3 Yes, there is. There is a piece of cheese and half a cake on the middle

shelf. 4 No, there is not. There is nothing on the fourth shelf. 5 Yes, there is. There is a bottle of milk on the bottom shelf.

D 1 (√) 2 (×) Not everybody has brown eyes. (Some people have black, blue, green or grey eyes.) 3 (×) Some people like snakes (because they are beautiful and interesting). 4 (√) 5 (×) Not everybody likes pizza. (Some people hate pizza because they do not like cheese or tomatoes.) 6 (×) Not all cows eat grass. (Some cows eat turnips.) 7 (×) Not all cars have four wheels. (Some cars/Reliant Robins have three wheels.)

18 I feel fine!

A 1 Is there anybody/anyone at home? No, there's nobody/no one at home. 2 Somebody/Someone is drinking my milk! 3 Has anybody/anyone got my bag? 4 Nobody/No one loves me because I'm ugly! 5 Somebody/Someone loves me – they send me flowers every week! 6 There isn't anybody/anyone in the shop. It's empty.

B They are talking about person 2, person 4 and person 5.

C Person 1 is short and fat. She is quite old. She has grey hair and big eyes. She has a long chin. Person 3 is a man. He has very little hair but he has a moustache. His mouth is straight and thin. He is short and he wears glasse

D For the answers, look at the pictures on page 147.

E My leg hurts! My eyes hurt! My back hurts! My nose hurts! My head hurts! My feet hurt! My teeth hurt! My left ear hurts! My right arm hurts! My chest hurts! My stomach hurts! My hand hurts! My toes hurt! My finger hurts! My ears hurt! My neck hurts!

F 1 Ms Down is 21 years old. She has a headache. Her eyes hurt and she often feels tired. 2 Peter East is 11 years old. He has earache/His ears hurt. 3 Mr Potter is 78 years old. His back, neck and arms hurt. 4 Miss Brown is 52 years old. Her stomach hurts/She has a stomach ache and her chest hurts.

19 Who were they?

A 1 In 1944 he was one year old. 2 In 1960 he was 17 years old. 3 – 4 He was at school in 1953. 5 He was in hospital in (November) 1948. 6 In May 1961 he was in Africa. 7 He was in France in 1964. 8 He was in London in 1973. 9 He was 35 years old in 1978.

B Reporter: Did you have breakfast this morning?
Joe: Yes, I did.
Reporter: What did you have for breakfast?
Joe: I had coffee, toast and jam.
Reporter: When did you have breakfast?
Joe: At seven o'clock.

Reporter: Where did you have it?
Joe: In the kitchen.

Reporter: Did you have breakfast this morning?
Sally: No, I didn't have any breakfast this morning. I was late for work.

Reporter: Did you have breakfast this morning?
Colin: Yes, I did.
Reporter: What did you have for breakfast?
Colin: I had tea and toast.
Reporter: When did you have breakfast?
Colin: At nine o'clock.
Reporter: Where did you have it?
Colin: In bed. I was ill.

Reporter: Did you have breakfast this morning?
Peter: Yes, I did.
Reporter: What did you have for breakfast?
Peter: I had sausages, eggs, tomatoes, toast, orange juice and coffee.
Reporter: Where did you have breakfast?
Peter: In the dining room.

D 1 Professor English talked from two o'clock to/until three o'clock. He talked for an hour. 2 The baby cried from half past one to/until four o'clock. It cried for two had a half hours. 3 Charlie played CDs from nine o'clock to/until half past eleven. He played CDs for two and a half hours. 4 James watched TV from quarter past six to/until twenty-five past seven. He watched TV for an hour and ten minutes. 5 Harry worked in California from 1 June to/until 1 September. He worked in California for three months. 6 Kit was ill from Monday morning to/until Wednesday night. She was ill for three days. 7 Brenda lived in London from 1973 to/until 1978. She lived in London for five years. 8 Tim cleaned the car from quarter past three to/until twenty past four. He cleaned the car for an hour and five minutes. 9 Amy played in the tree house from ten o'clock to/until three o'clock. She played in the tree house for five hours. 10 Mr Duncan played his double bass from half past seven to/until eleven o'clock. He played his double bass for three and a half hours.

E
1 Mahatma Gandhi was a famous Indian statesman. He was born in India in 1869. He lived in London and South Africa for many years. He came back to India in 1918. He died in India in 1948.
2 Marco Polo was a famous traveller. He was born in Italy in 1254. He travelled to China with his father in 1271. He lived in China for many years. He came home to Italy, and he died in Italy in 1324.
3 Wolfgang Amadeus Mozart was a famous composer. He was born in Austria in 1756. He composed his first piece of music at the age of 5. He travelled with his father and sister to Germany, France, England and Italy. He married in 1782. He and his wife had six children, but four of their children died. Mozart composed hundreds of pieces of music, but he was always poor. He died in 1791.

F 1 The book shop is open from 9 a.m. to 5.30 p.m. It closes for lunch at 12.30 p.m. for an hour. It opens again at 1.30 p.m. and it closes again at 5.30 p.m. 2 The dress shop is open from 9.30 a.m. to 5.30 p.m. It closes for lunch at 12.30 p.m. for an hour and a half. It opens again at 2 p.m. and closes again at 5.30 p.m. 3 The shoe shop is open from 9 a.m. to 5 p.m. It closes for lunch at 1 p.m. for an hour and a half. It opens again at 2.30 p.m. and closes again at 5 p.m. 4 The newsagent is open from 7.30 a.m. to 5.30 p.m. It does not close for lunch.

G Mr Duncan wanted to go to the station. He needed to catch the 6.30 train to London. He phoned Barbara. "Can you take me to the station?" he asked. "Of course," answered Barbara.
She arrived at Mr Duncan's house at 5 30 a.m. in her taxi. She opened the taxi door and helped him with his double bass. They arrived at the station and Barbara parked her taxi in the car park. She waved goodbye to Mr Duncan. Mr Duncan arrived in London. He played in a concert, then he had dinner with the other musicians. He was very tired.

20 Once upon a time

A 1 The dog caught a rabbit, then it ate it. 2 Brenda wrote a letter and sent it to her mother. 3 Tim made a cup of tea and drank it. 4 Amy bought a pair of red sunglasses and wore them at school. 5 The bird bit me, then it flew away. 6 Harry built a bridge in Singapore, then he left Singapore and went to Dubai. 7 James fell off his bicycle and broke his nose. 8 Barbara drove to Mr Duncan's house and took him to a concert. 9 Charlie felt ill, so he went to the doctor. 10 Charlie taught Amy to play football and bought her a pair of football boots.

B 1 Eyke is near Woodbridge and it is not very far from Ipswich. 2 Tunstall is near Bromeswell, but it is a long way from London. 3 Martlesham is very near Ipswich and not far from Woodbridge. 4 Tunstall, Melton and Bromeswell are all very near Eyke, but they are a long way from London.

C 1 She sat in the garden and smelt the flowers. 2 The firemen rang the bell, then drove their fire engine to the fire. 3 James ate two pizzas and drank a bottle of lemonade, then he felt sick. 4 Charlie fell off his bicycle and hurt his arm. 5 I broke a plate, so I bought a new one. 6 The bird took a piece of bread and flew away. 7 Barbara wrote a long letter to Tim and sent it in a big white envelope. 8 The cat chased a rabbit and caught it. Then he took it to the King.

21 What are you going to do?

A Charlie lost his football boots. He came home from school by bus. Charlie telephoned the bus station. "Did anybody find a pair of football boots on the Number 23 bus?" he asked. The man went away for a few minutes. "Yes," he said, "Someone found them." Charlie went to the bus station on foot. He gave the man his name and address and the man gave him the football boots . . . Then Charlie lost them again!

B heated; buttered; cut; put; added; sprinkled; beat; mixed; poured; left; cooked; took; asked; ate

C 1 He is going to clean his teeth. 2 He is going to go to Paris. 3 Yes, she is. 4 He is going to read the newspaper. 5 No, he is not. He is going to open a tin. 6 No, he is not. He is going to play tennis. 7 No, he is not. He is going to play the guitar. 8 She is going to go to a concert. 9 She is going to eat a cake. 10 Yes, he is.

D 1 Bill: I'm going to be a doctor. I'm going to help people. 2 Connie: I'm going to be an artist. I'm going to paint beautiful pictures. 3 Tommy: I'm going to be a teacher. I'm going to teach little children the alphabet. 4 Eleanor: I'm going to be an engineer. I'm going to build roads and bridges. 5 Mike: I'm going to be a secretary. I'm going to work in an office. 6 Vicky: I'm going to be a film star. I'm going to make exciting films. 7 Sam: I'm going to be a cook. I'm going to cook wonderful meals for famous people. 8 John: I'm going to be a fireman. I'm going to drive a fire engine.

22 I'm still reading

A 1 Barbara has been in the shower for twenty minutes. 2 Harry has been an engineer for a long time. 3 The old man has been in hospital for six weeks. 4 Amy has been in her tree house for three hours. 5 Rosy has lived in Eyke for twenty years.

B 1 Harry has been in the garden since 2 o'clock. 2 Brenda has been a secretary since 1982. 3 Tim has worked in an office since the age of 18. 4 Fred has had Jimmy since 1985. 5 Max has been asleep since 3 a.m.

C 1 Fred's dog has been ill for two days. 2 Charlie has been asleep since 10 o'clock. 3 Mary and Jack have been married for 21 years. 4 Paul and Sarah have been married since 1989. 5 Amy has been at home since 4 o'clock. 6 James has been at school for three hours. 7 Max and Kit have been in the kitchen since this afternoon. 8 Professor English has been awake since 5 a.m. 9 Brenda and Harry have lived in this house for 12 years. 10 Della has had this job since 1992. 11 Tim has been in the bath for 10 minutes. 12 Barbara has been in the shower since 6 o'clock.

D 1 We have been working here for 12 years. 2 Barbara has been painting her fingernails since 5 o'clock. 3 Harry has been waiting for Brenda for 20 minutes. 4 Kit has been playing the fiddle for two hours. 5 Max and Kit have been cooking since 2 o'clock. 6 Charlie has been reading a book for half an hour. 7 Brenda has been cleaning the kitchen since 12 o'clock. 8 Fred has been playing with his dog for an hour and a half. 9 It has been raining since Tuesday morning. 10 It has been snowing for three hours.

E 1 No, she has not. 2 Yes, she is. 3 Yes, he has. 4 Yes, she is. 5 No, she has not. 6 Yes, she has. 7 No, she has not. 8 No, she has not. 9 Yes, she is. 10 No, she has not. 11 Yes, she is. 12 No, she has not.

F I've already read it. I've already done them. I've already read it. No, I haven't read it yet.

Verbs

Present		**Past**		**Perfect**	

Regular verbs: example

I/you/we/they	jump	*I/you/we/they/*		*I/you/we/they*	have jumped
he/she/it	jumps	*he/she/it*	jumped	*he/she/it*	has jumped

to be

I	am	*I/he/she/it*	was	*I/you/we/they*	have been
you/we/they	are	*you/we/they*	were	*he/she/it*	has been
he/she/it	is				

to have

I/you/we/they	have	*I/you/we/they/*		*I/you/we/they*	have had
he/she/it	has	*he/she/it*	had	*he/she/it*	has had

Other irregular verbs

beat/beats	beat	beaten
begin/begins	began	begun
bite/bites	bit	bitten
blow/blows	blew	blown
break/breaks	broke	broken
bring/brings	brought	brought
build/builds	built	built
buy/buys	bought	bought
can	could	
catch/catches	caught	caught
come/comes	came	come
cost/costs	cost	cost
cry/cries	cried	cried
cut/cuts	cut	cut
dig/digs	dug	dug
do/does	did	done
draw/draws	drew	drawn
drink/drinks	drank	drunk
drive/drives	drove	driven
eat/eats	ate	eaten
fall/falls	fell	fallen
fly/flies	flew	flown
freeze/freezes	froze	frozen

Present	Past	Perfect
get/gets	got	got
give/gives	gave	given
go/goes	went	gone (*or* been)
grow/grows	grew	grown
hear/hears	heard	heard
hurt/hurts	hurt	hurt
know/knows	knew	known
leave/leaves	left	left
lose/loses	lost	lost
make/makes	made	made
meet/meets	met	met
pay/pays	paid	paid
put/puts	put	put
read/reads	read	read
ride/rides	rode	ridden
ring/rings	rang	rung
run/runs	ran	run
say/says	said	said
see/sees	saw	seen
sell/sells	sold	sold
send/sends	sent	sent
sing/sings	sang	sung
sit/sits	sat	sat
sleep/sleeps	slept	slept
smell/smells	smelt	smelt
speak/speaks	spoke	spoken
spend/spends	spent	spent
stand/stands	stood	stood
take/takes	took	taken
teach/teaches	taught	taught
tell/tells	told	told
think/thinks	thought	thought
wear/wears	wore	worn
win/wins	won	won
write/writes	wrote	written

Index

Grammar items and words found only in instructions for exercises are in bold.
adj = adjective; adv = adverb; comp = comparative; n = noun; sup = superlative; v = verb